Master Mandala

Copyright: Published in the United States by Beverly Rosa
Published December 2016
ISBN-13: 978-1541298460
ISBN-10: 1541298462

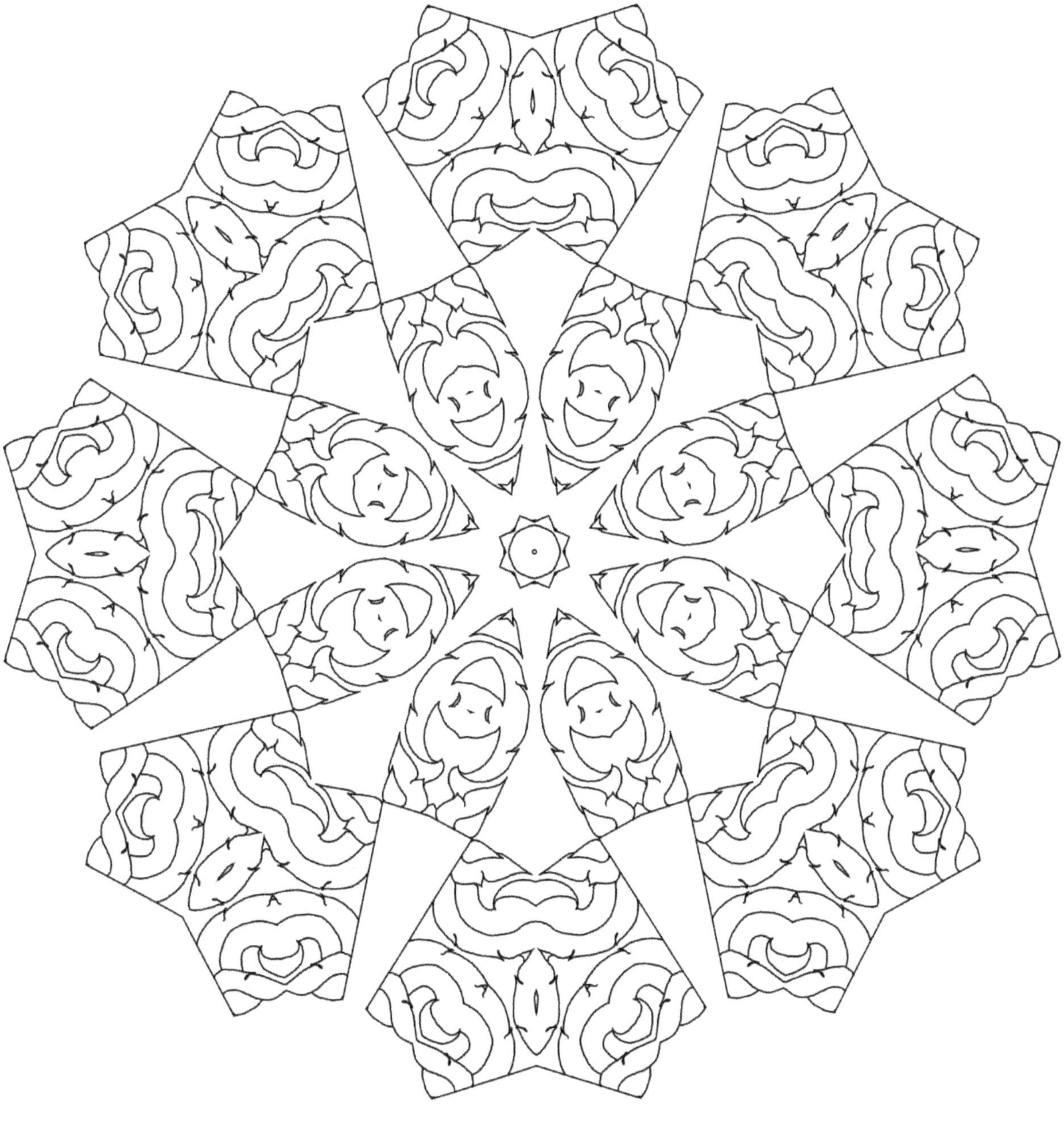

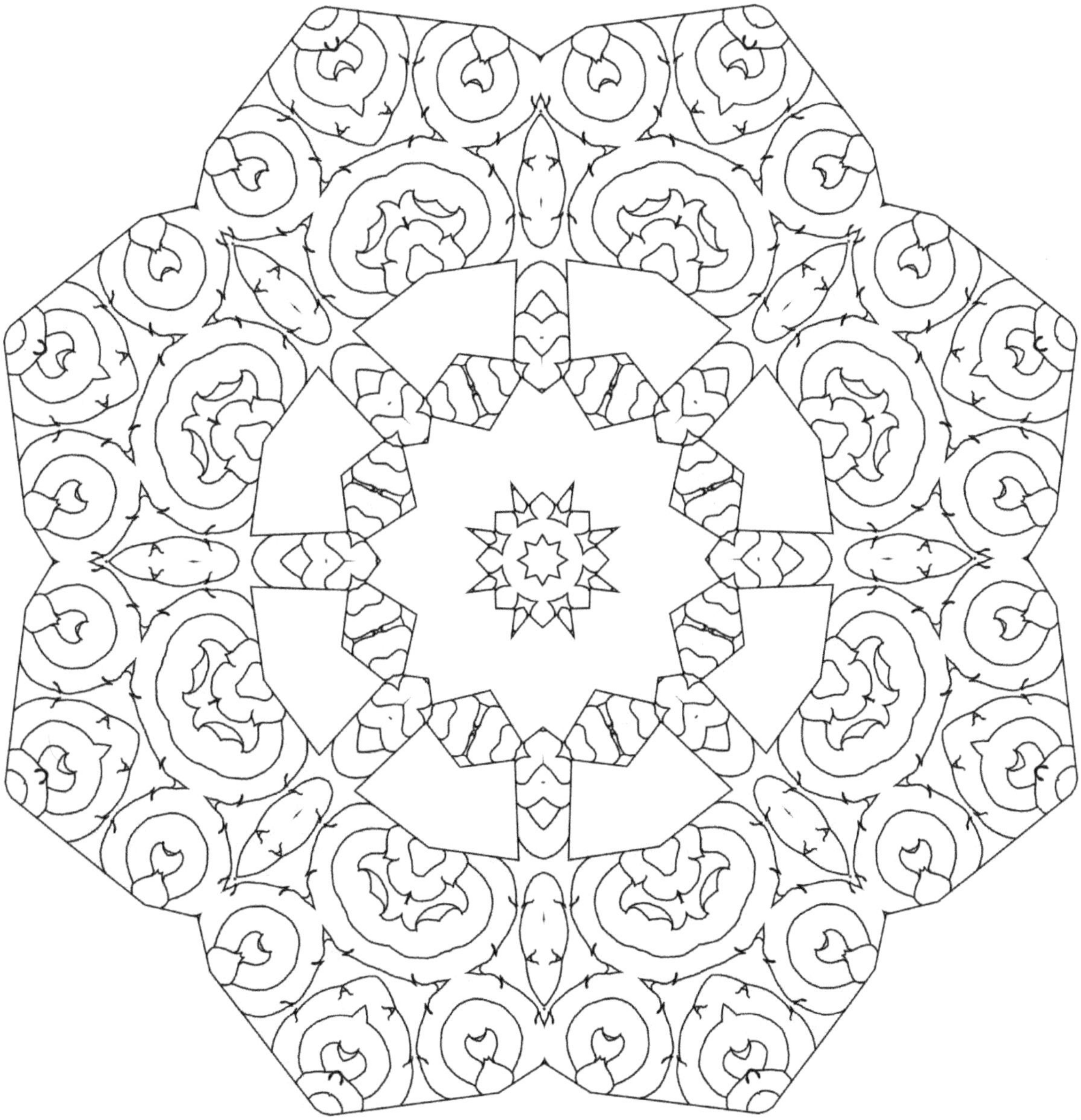

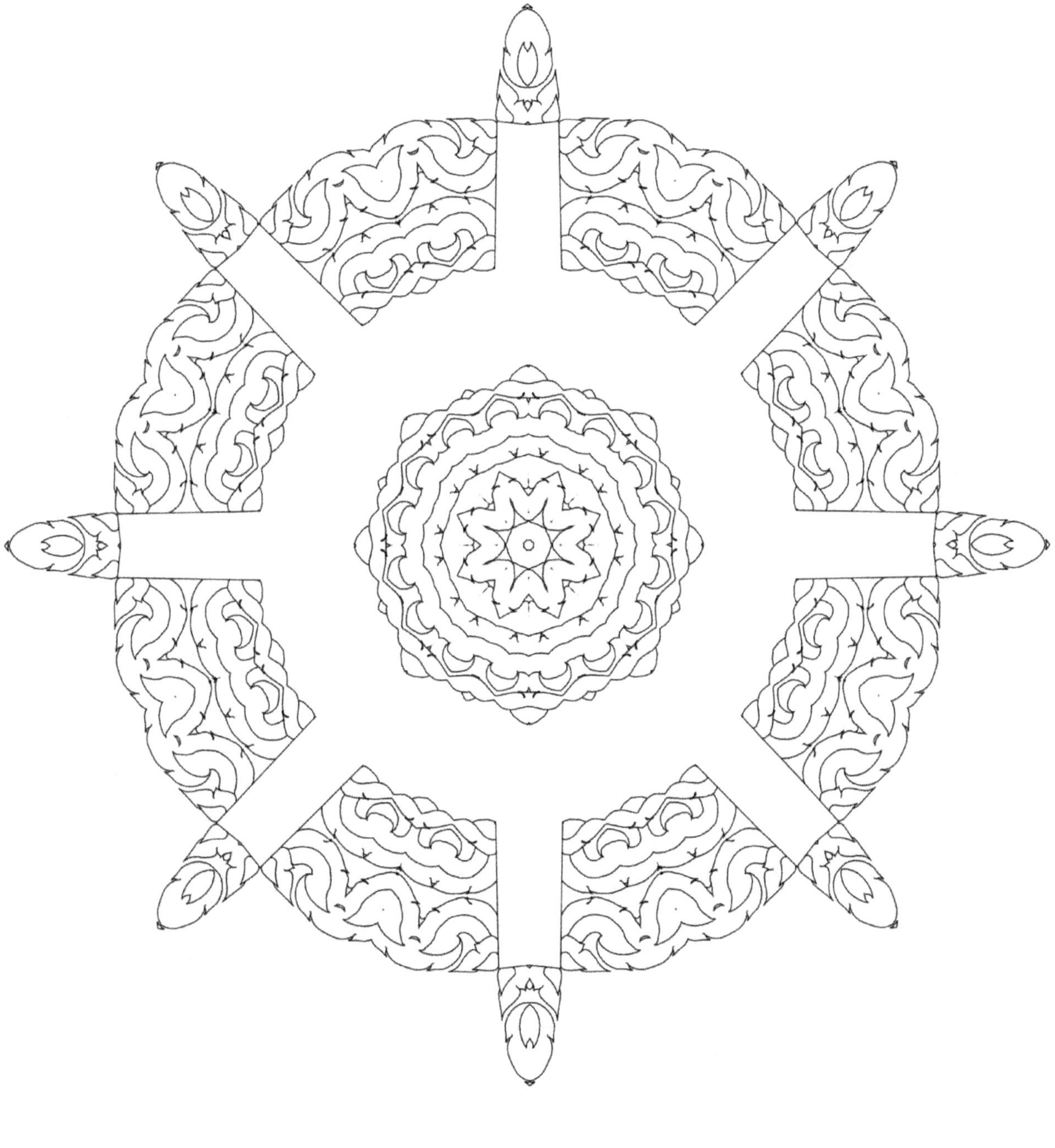

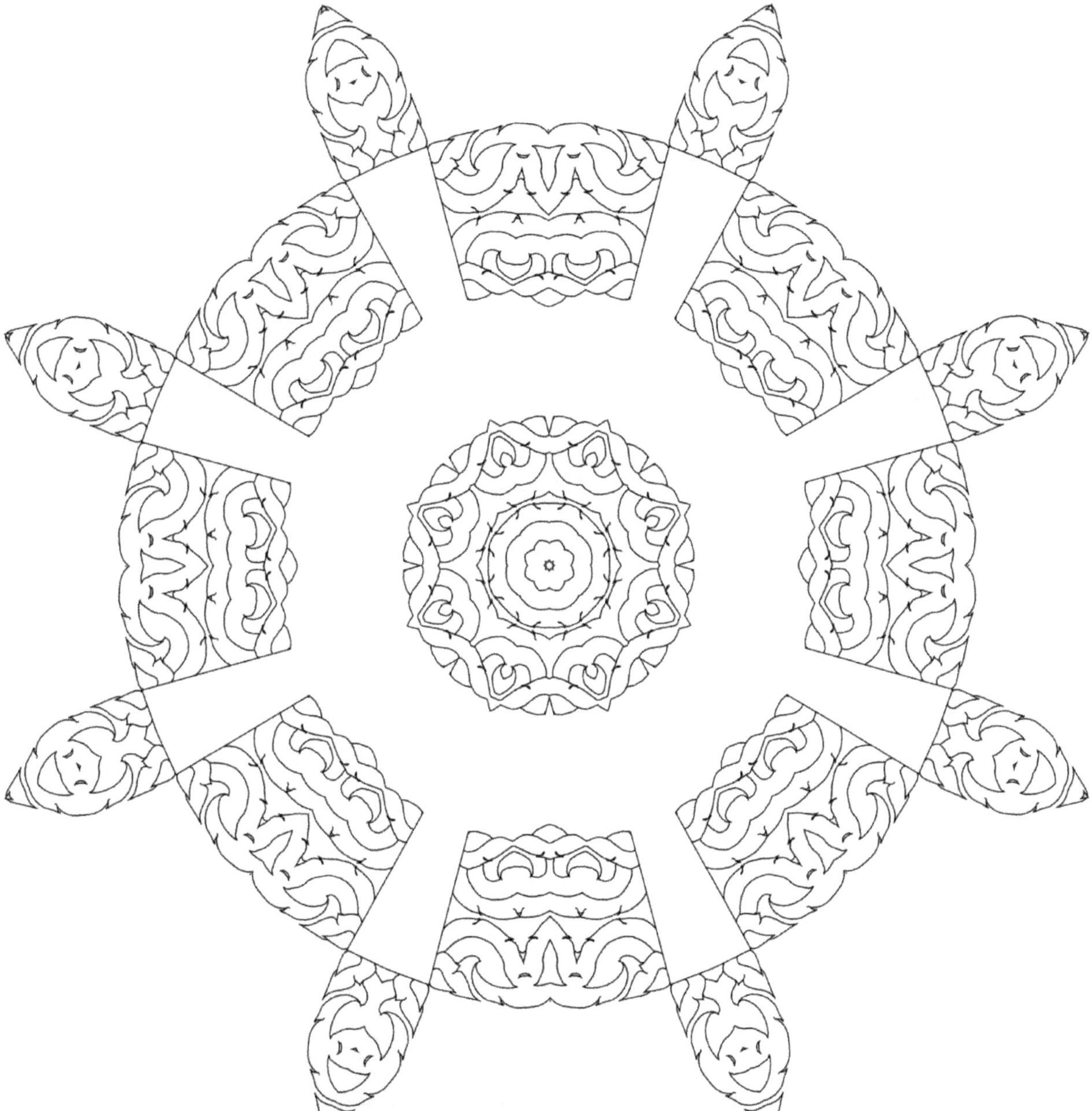

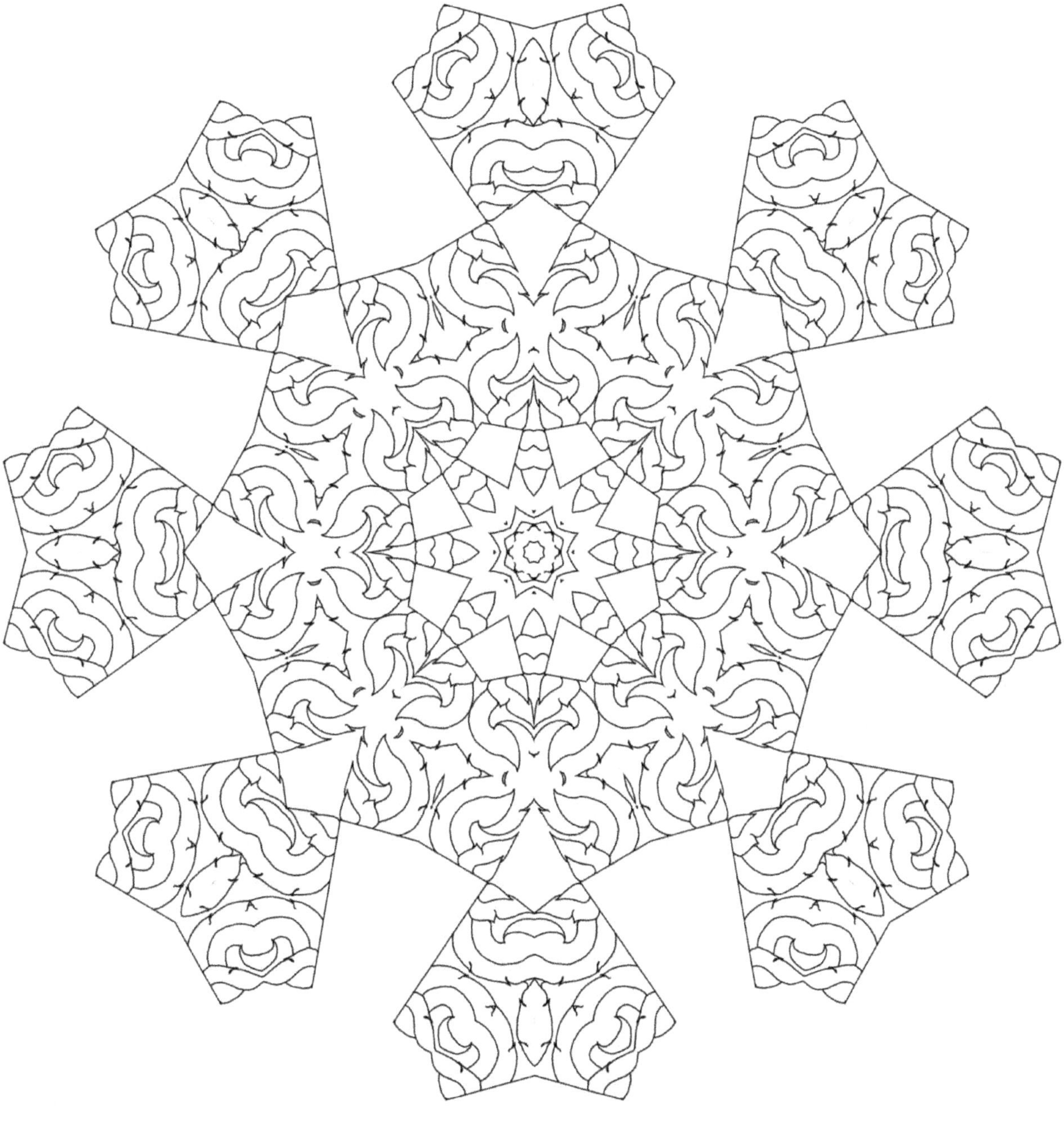

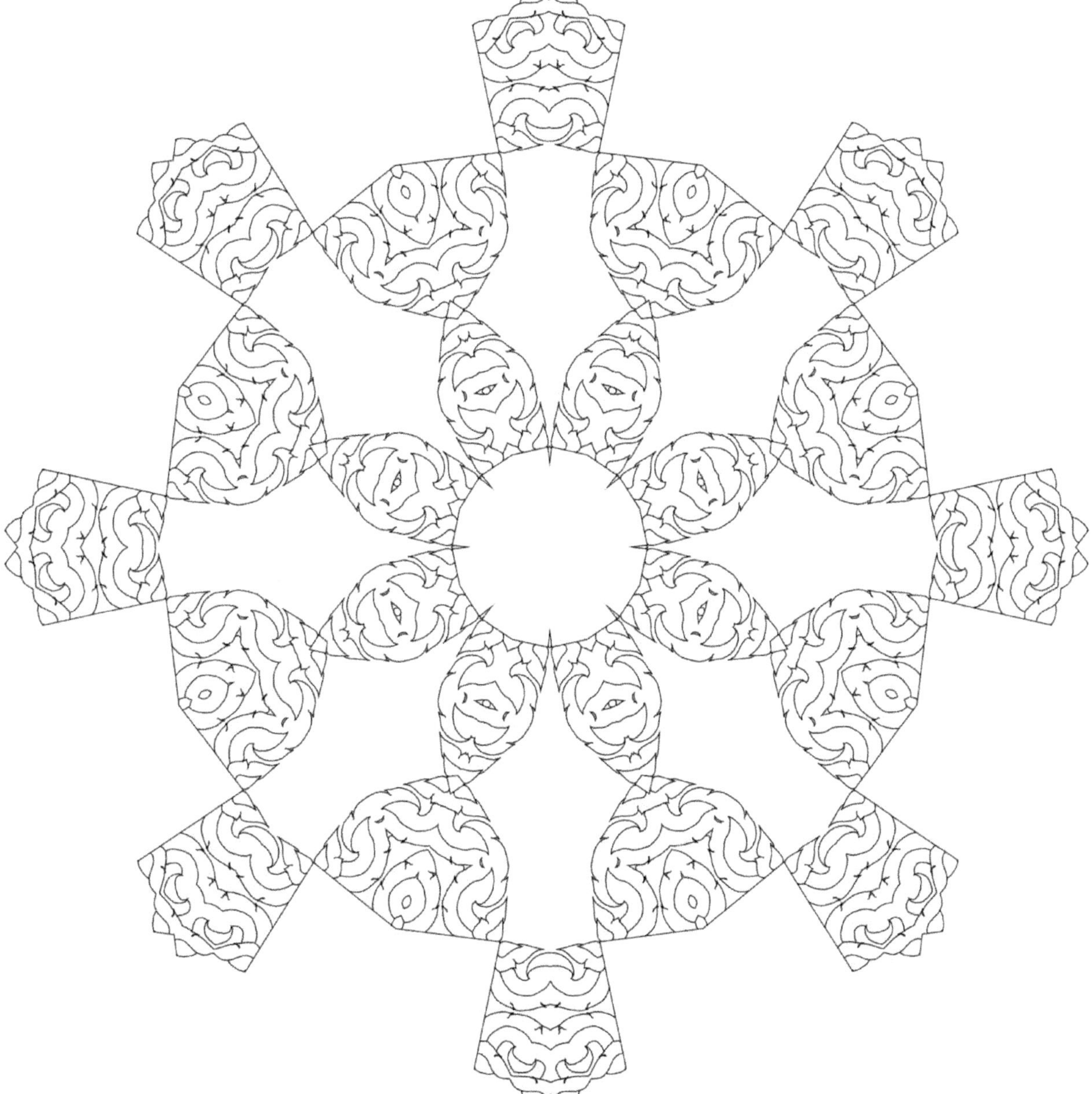

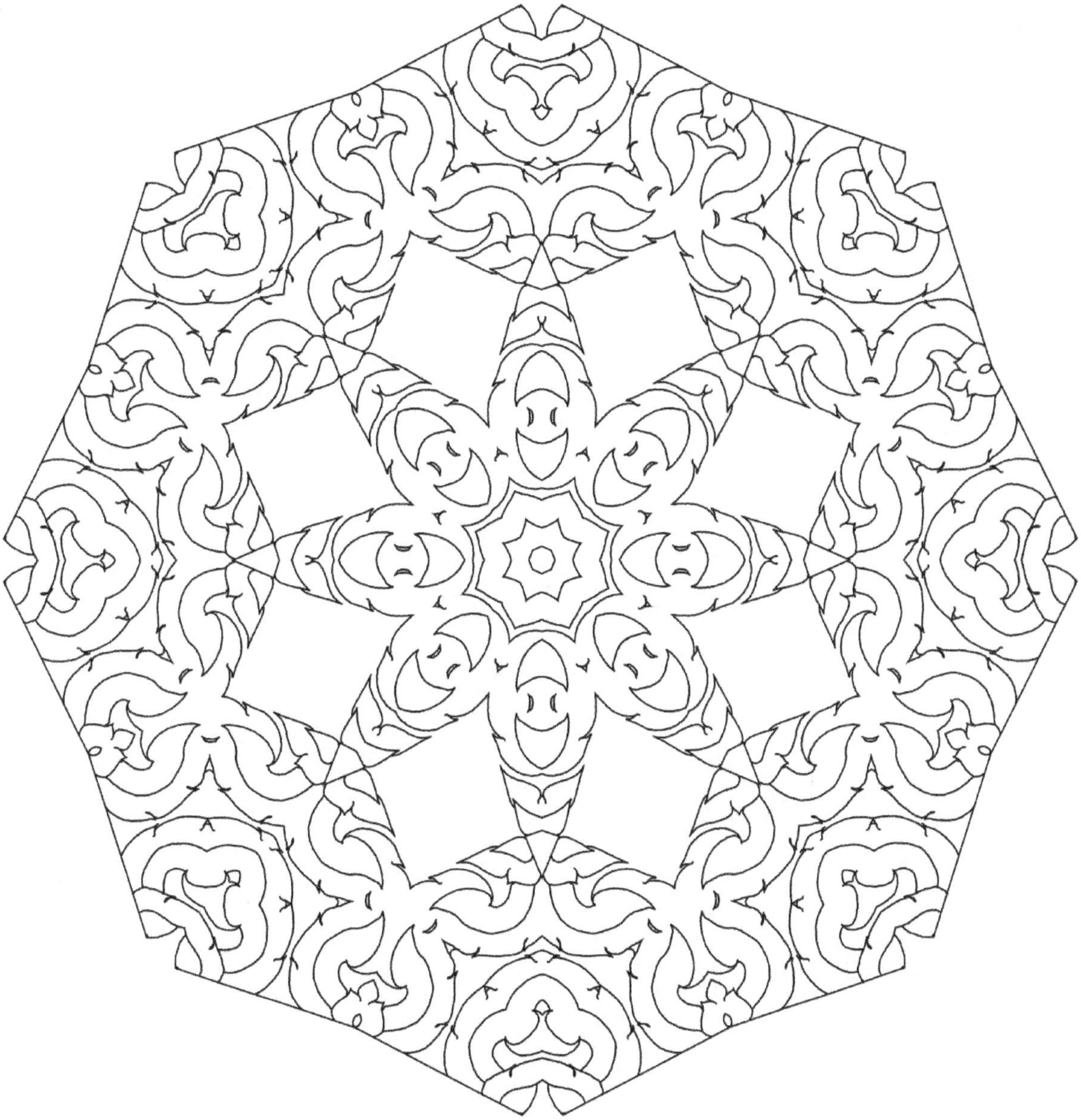

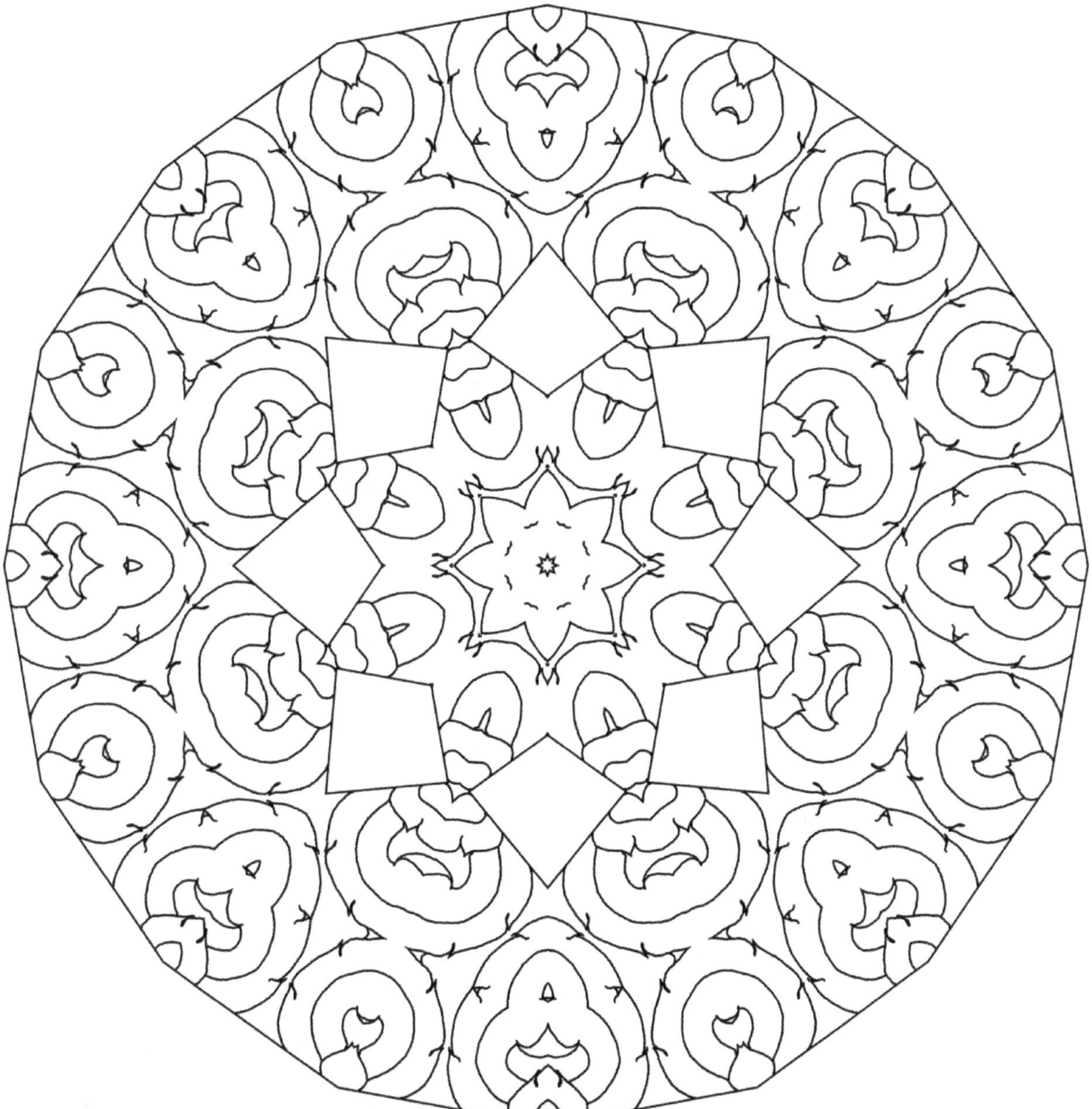

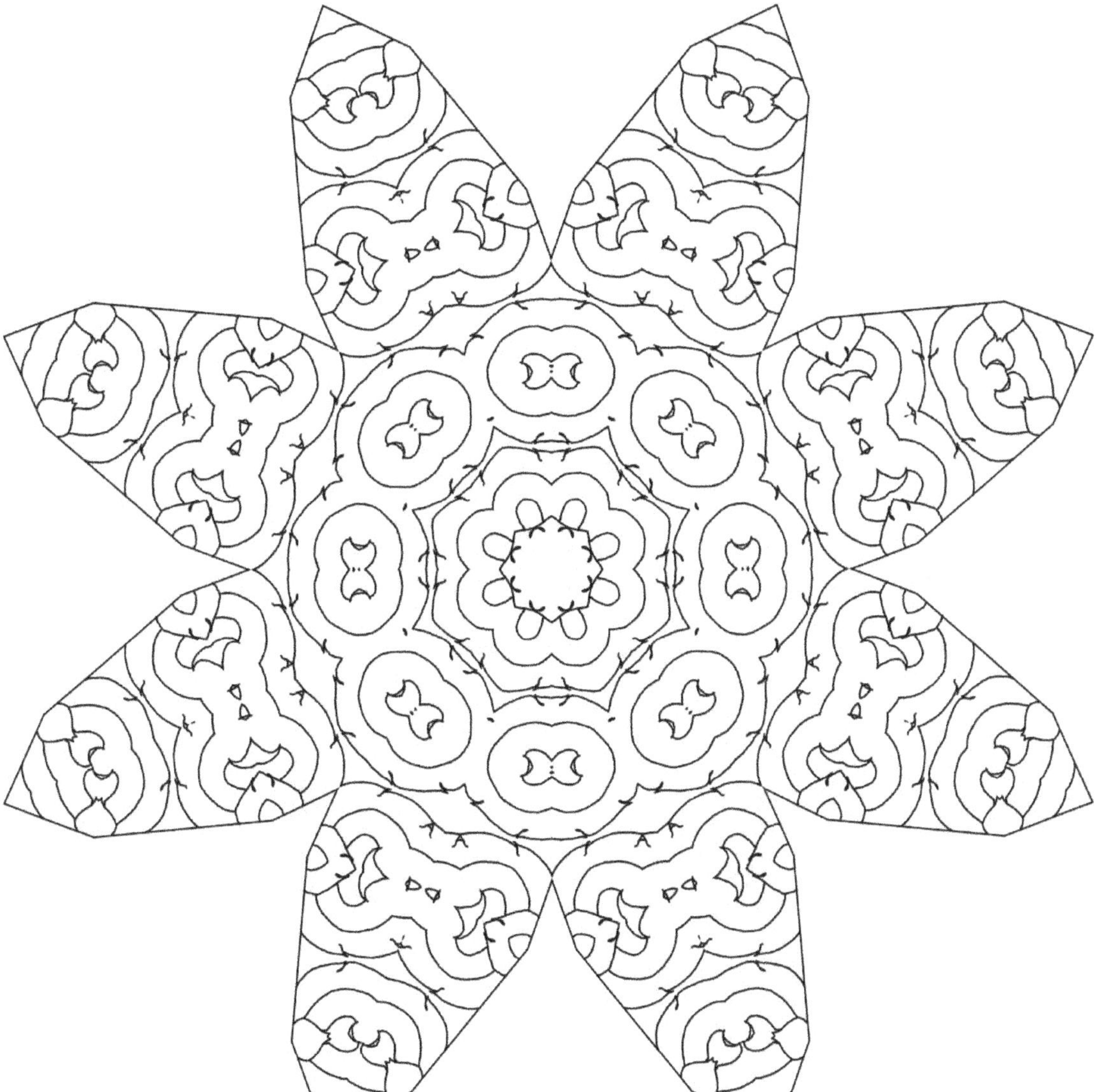

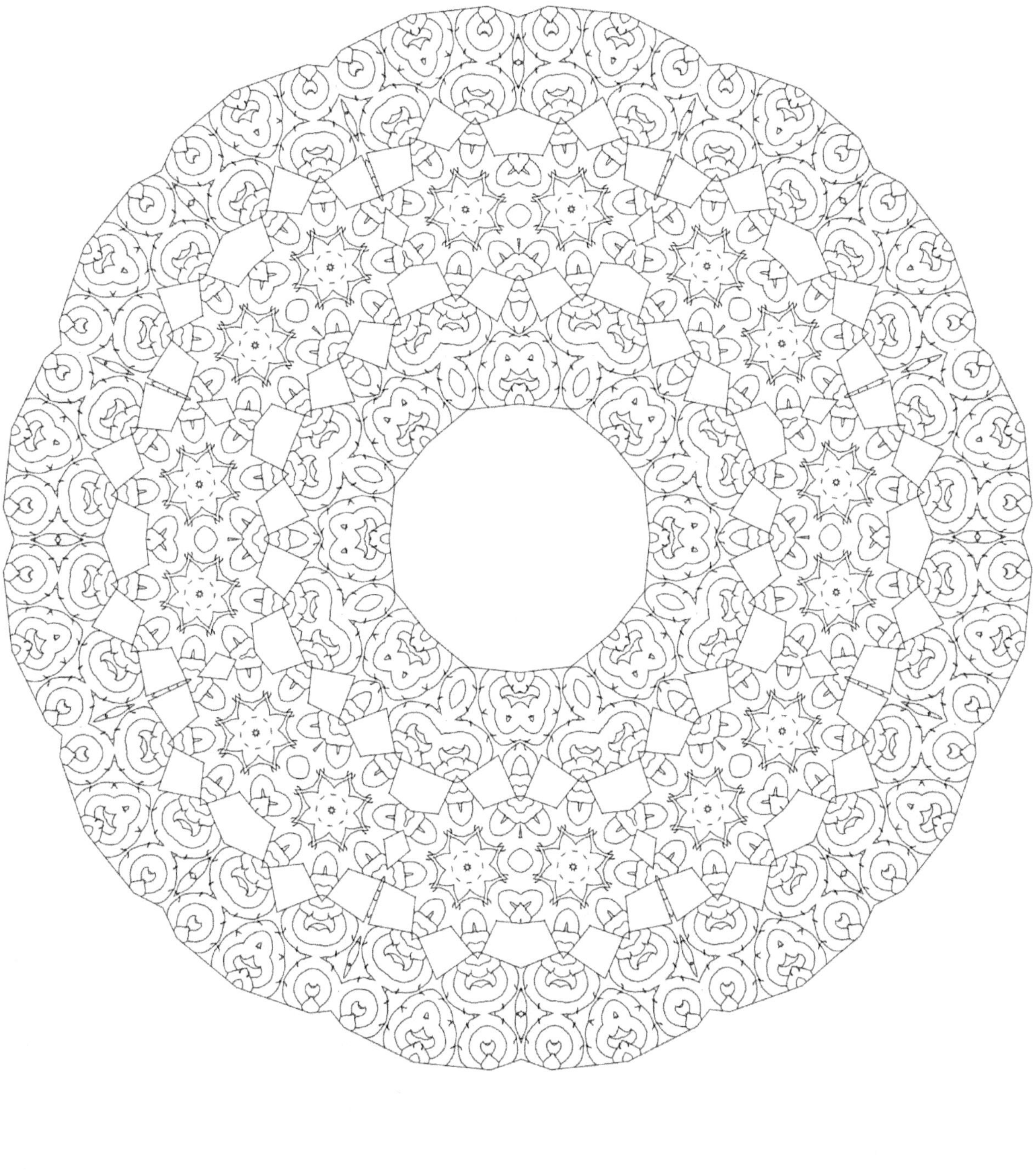

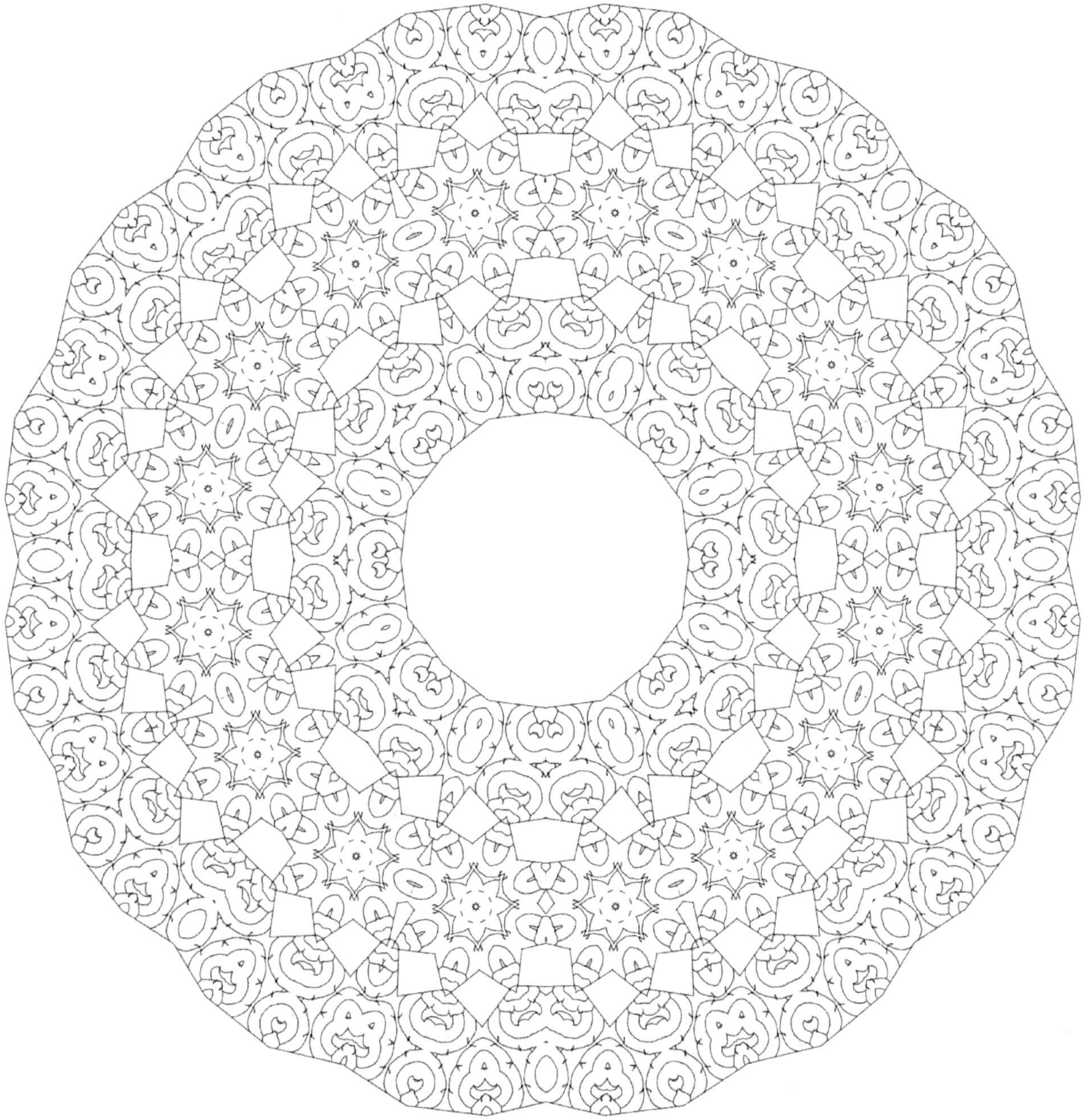

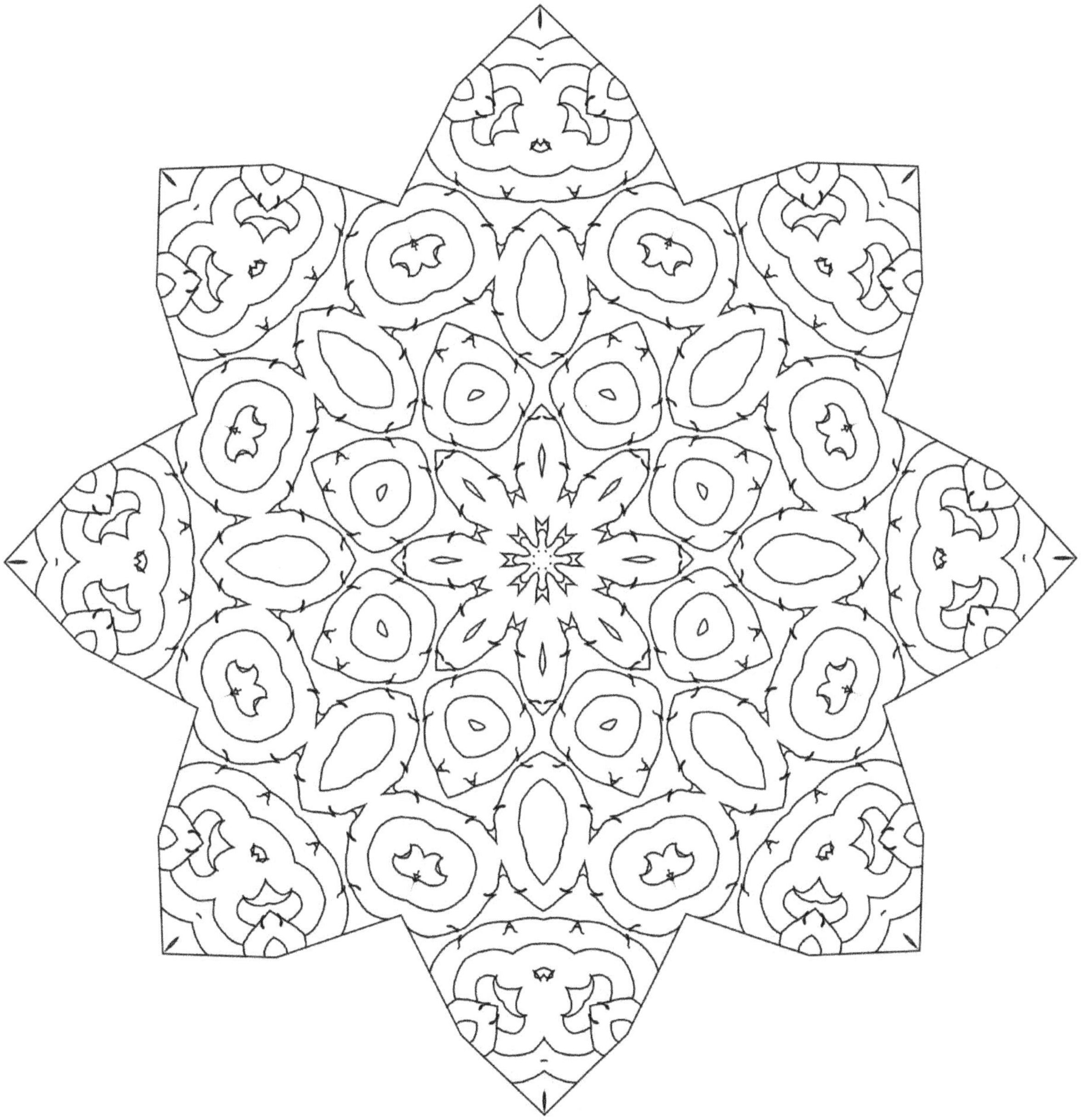

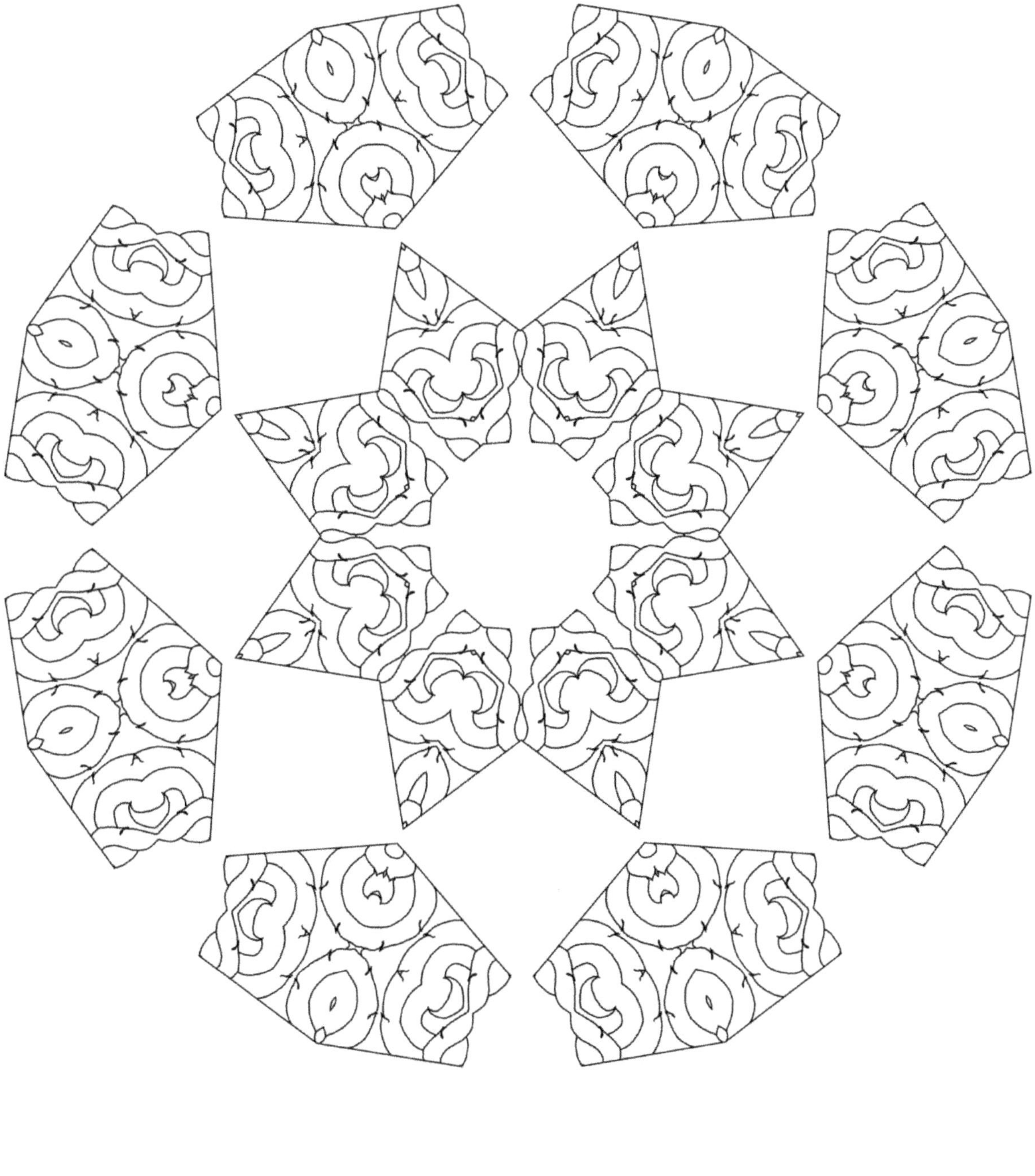

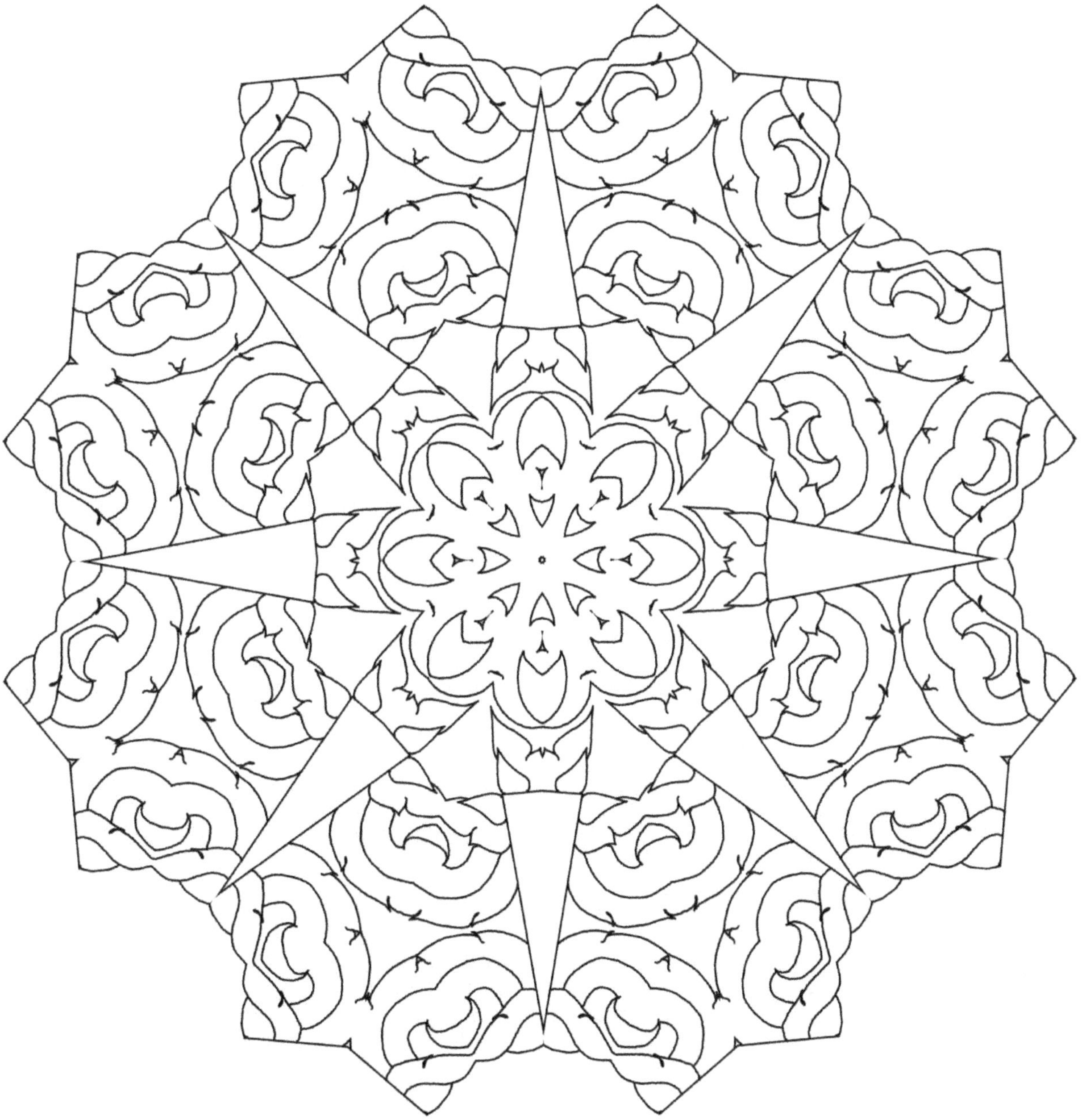

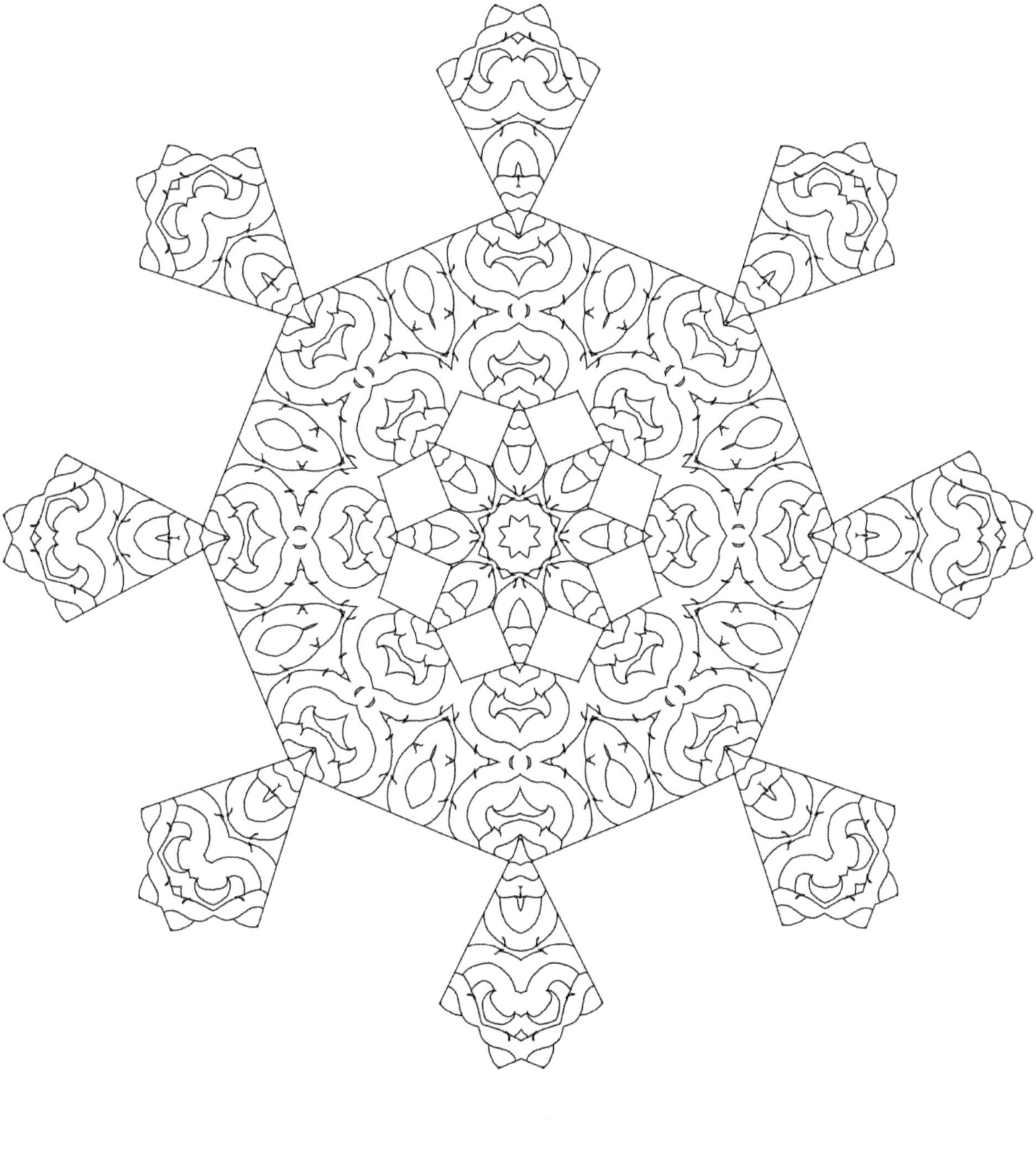

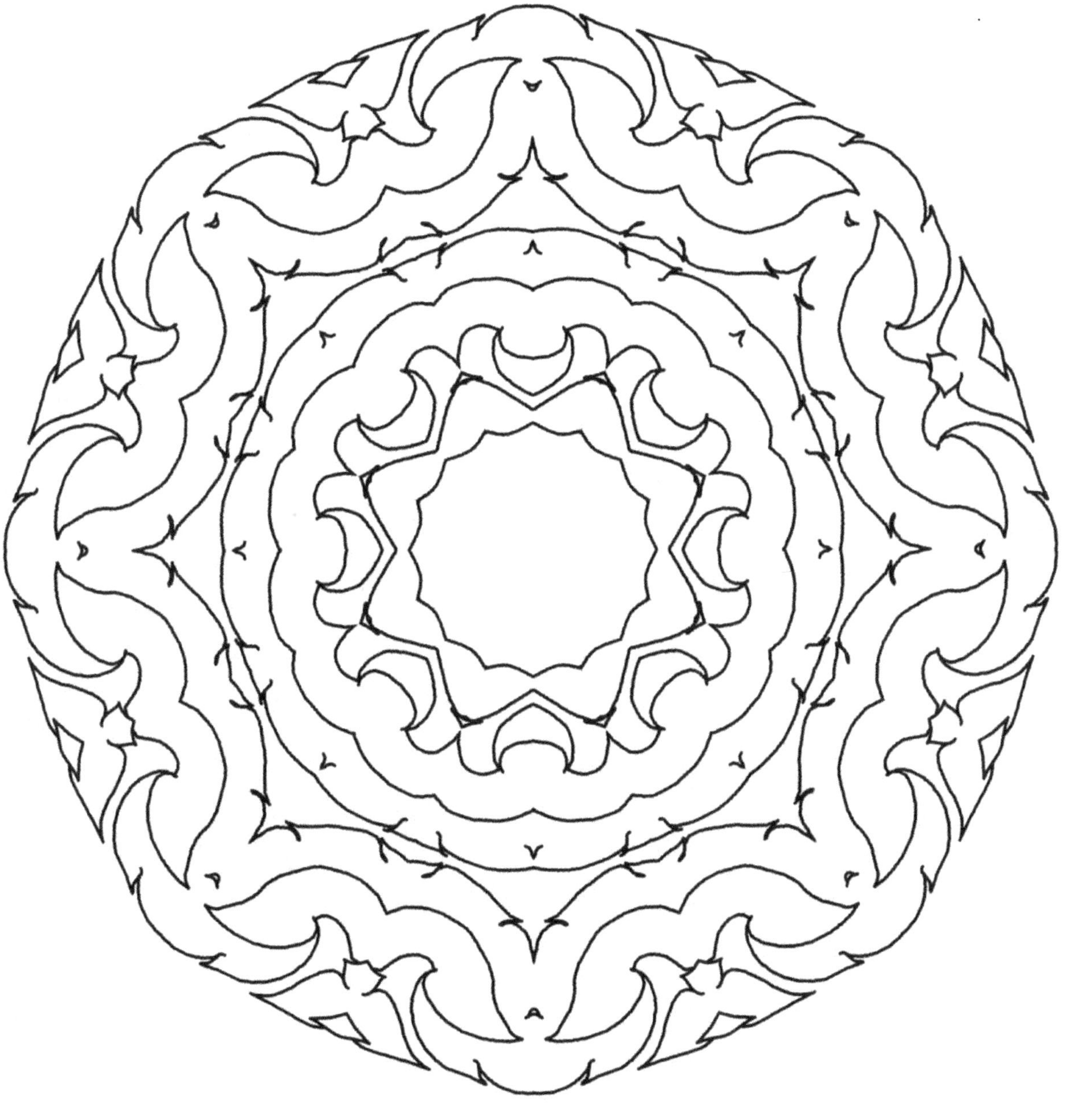

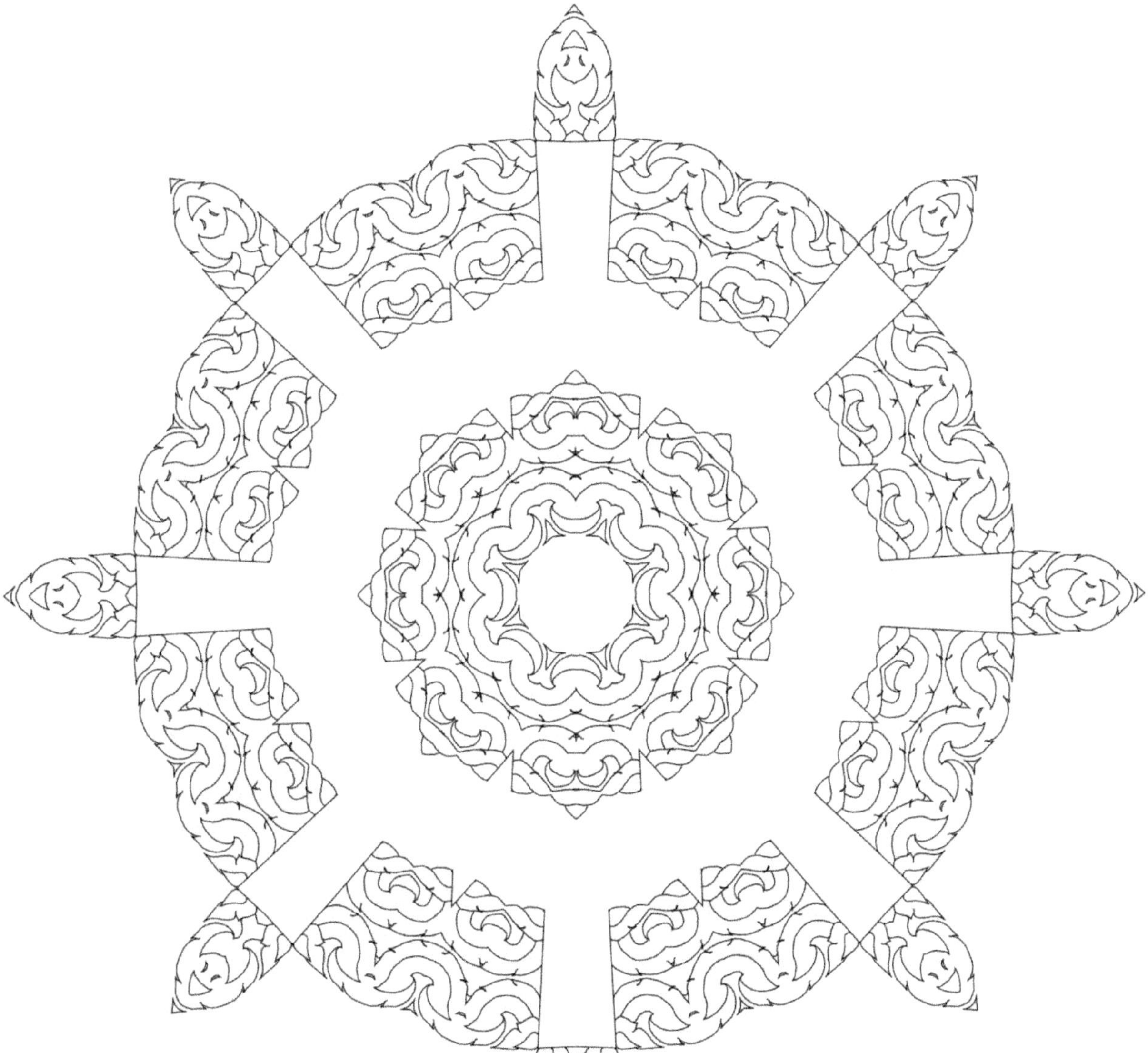

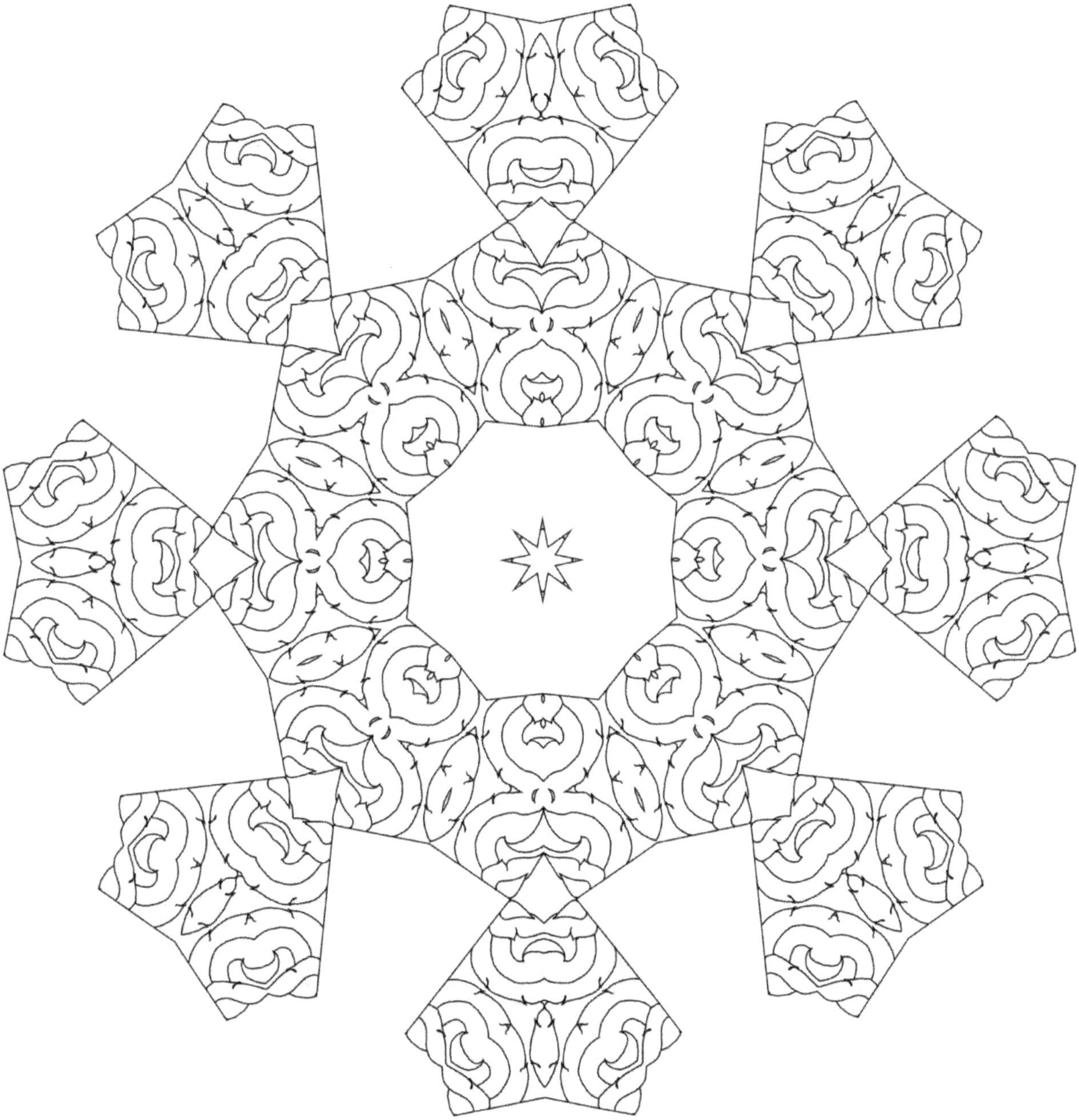

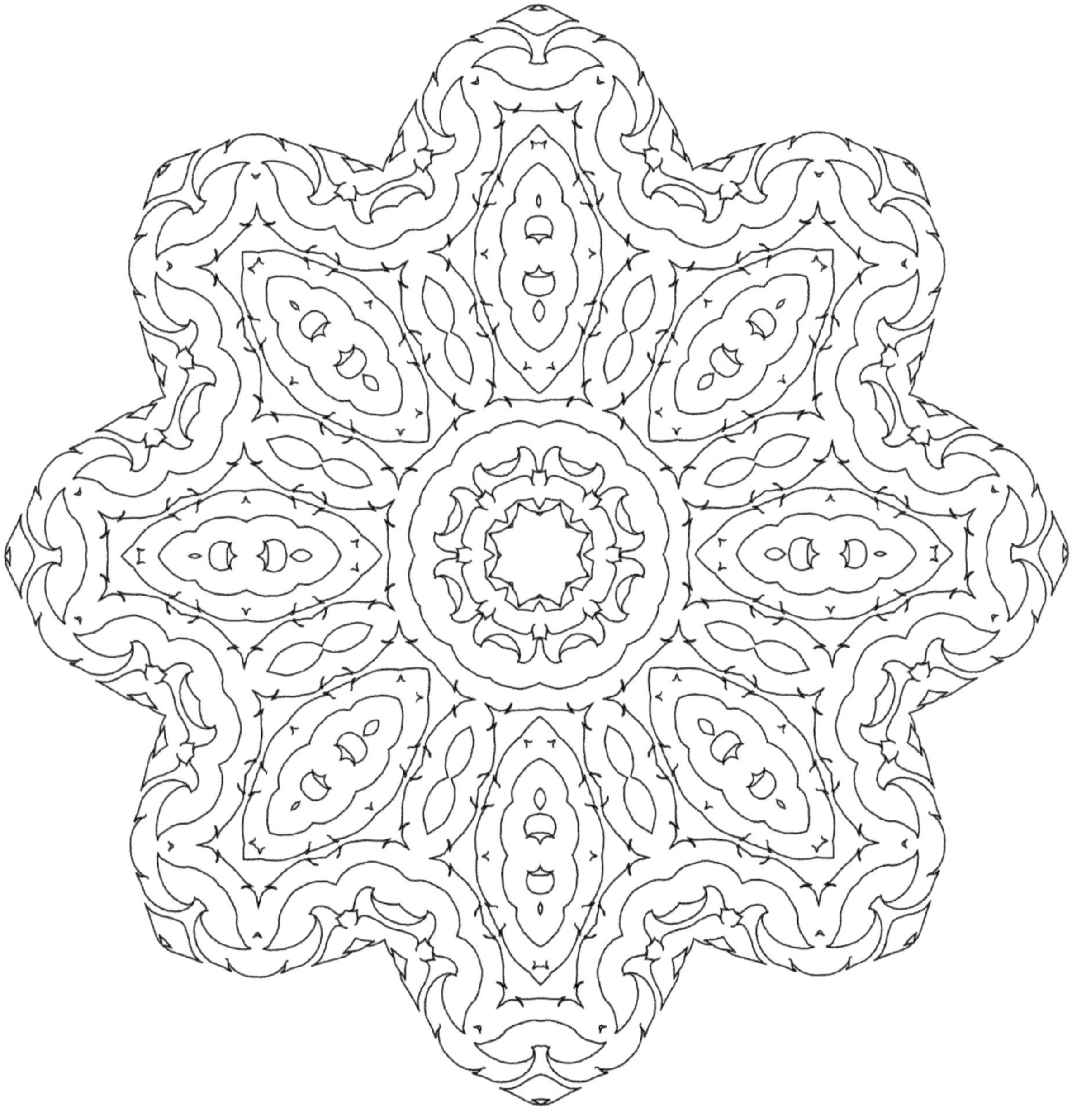

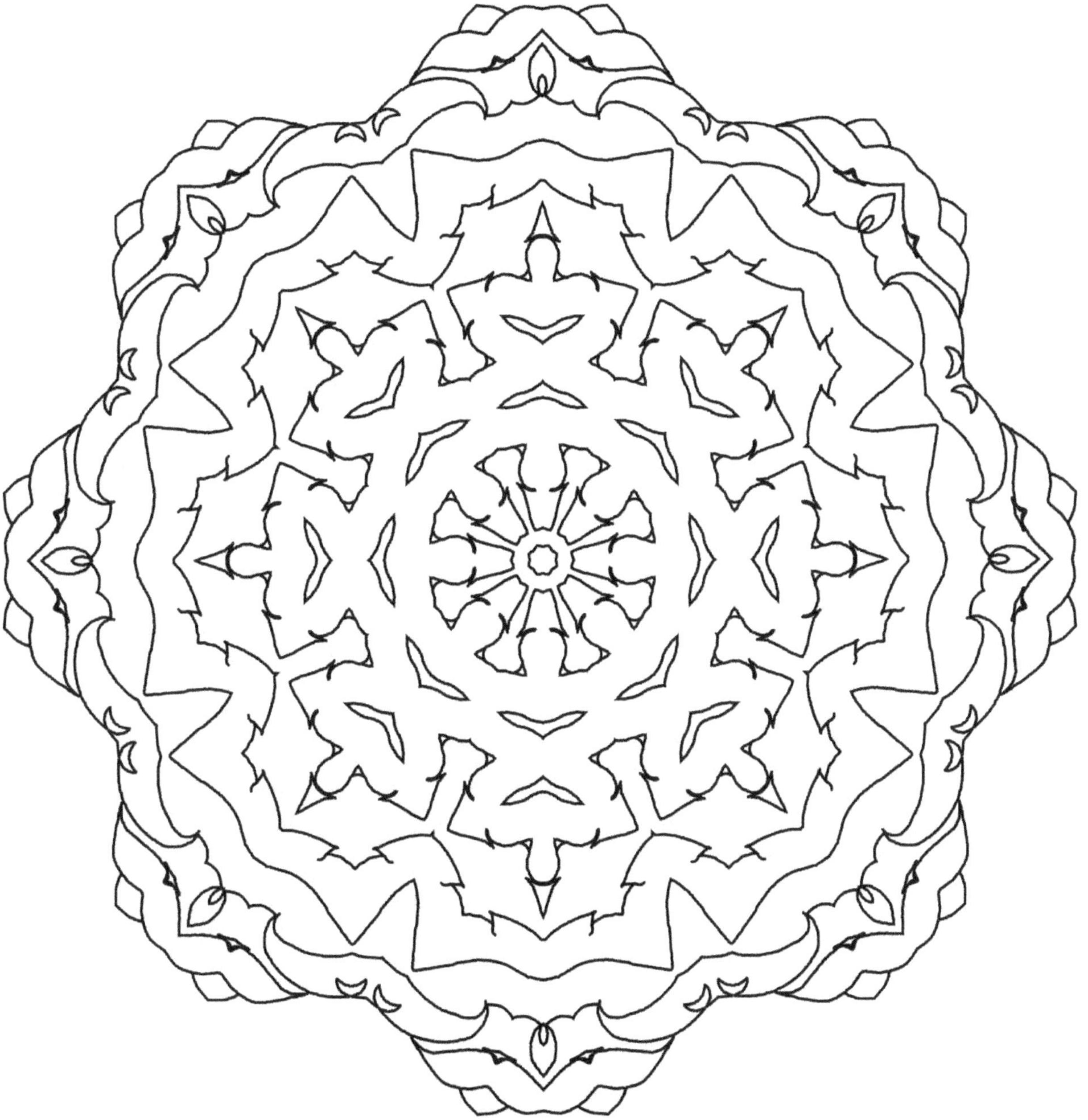

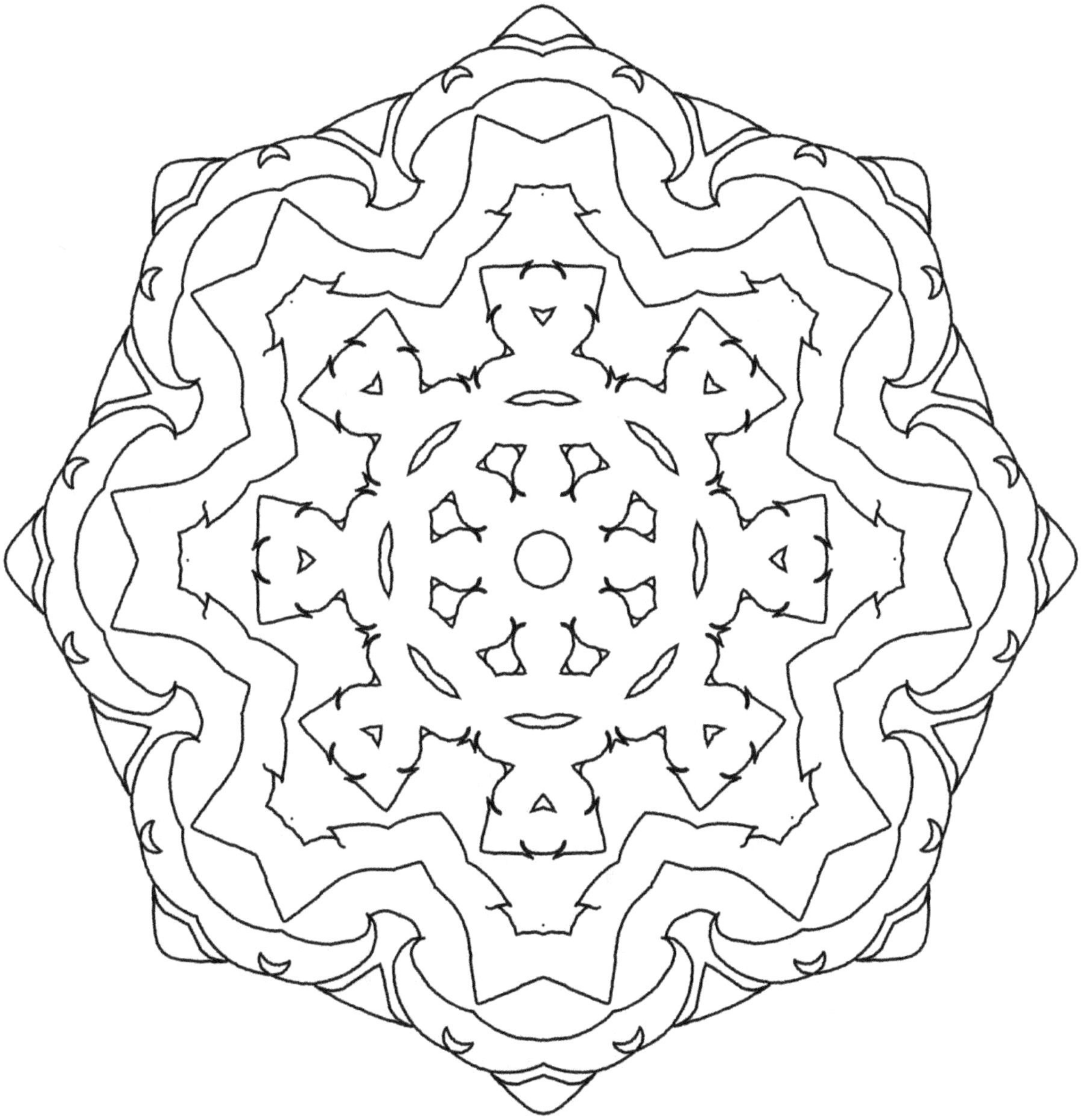

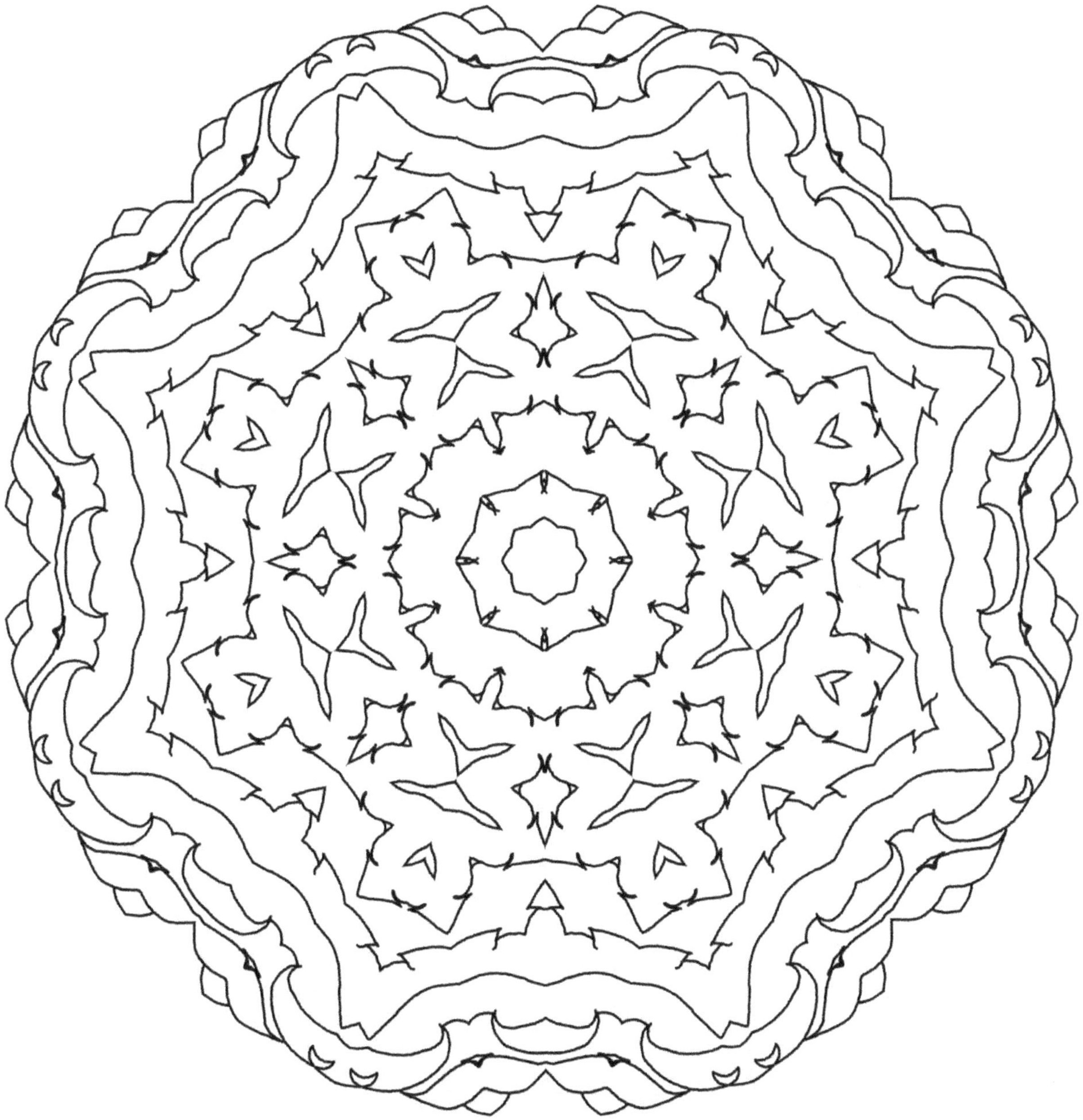

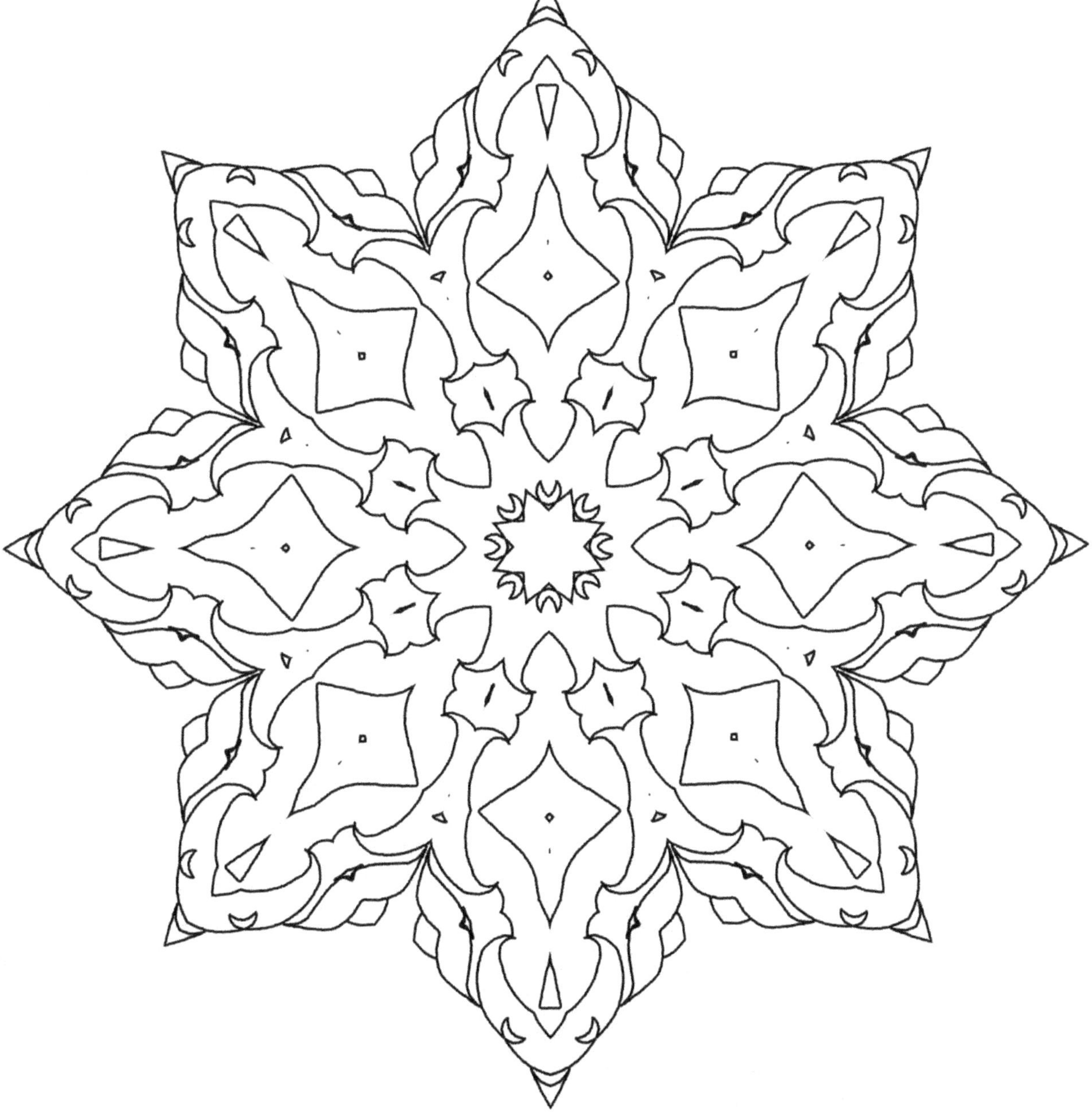

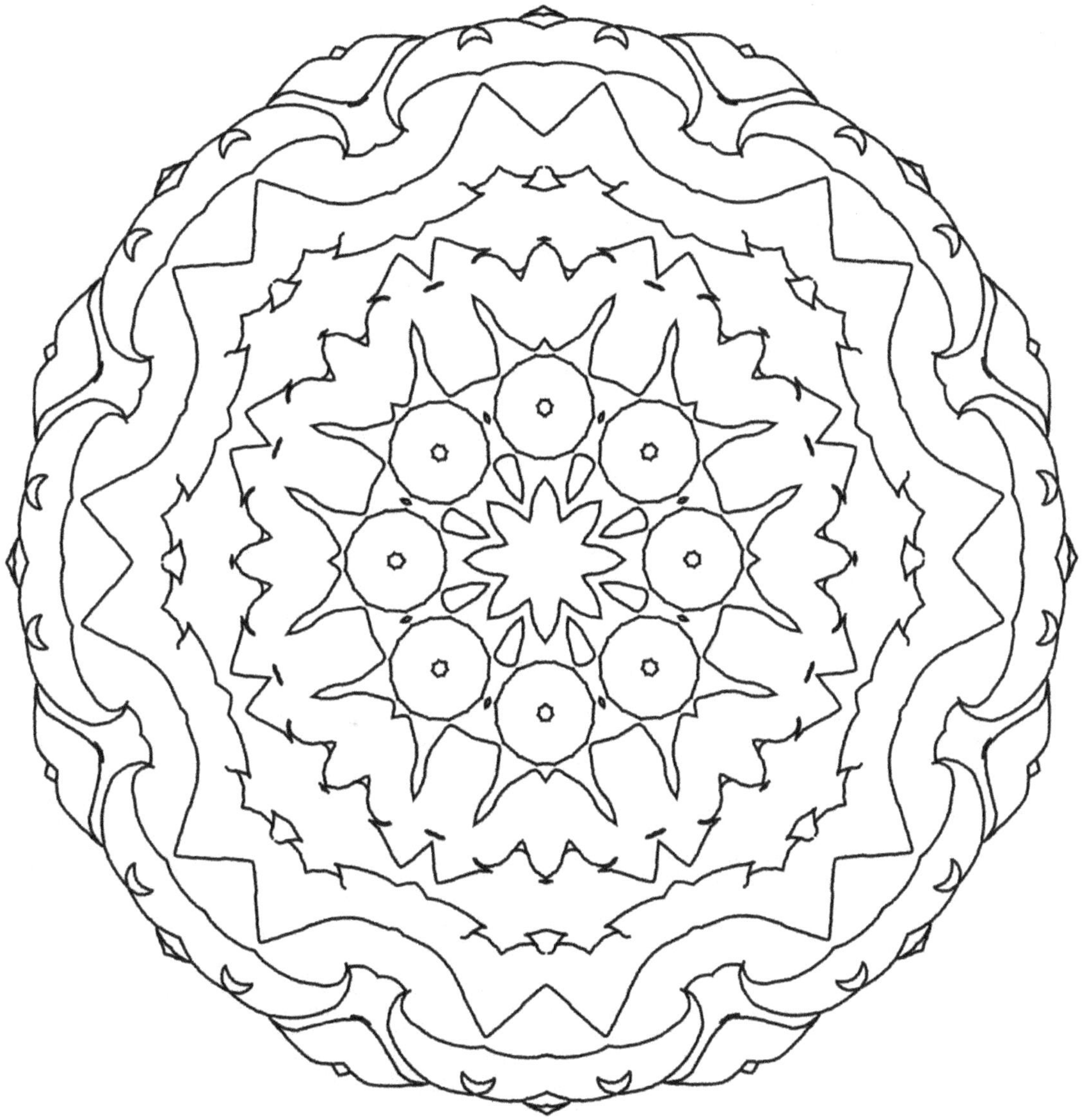

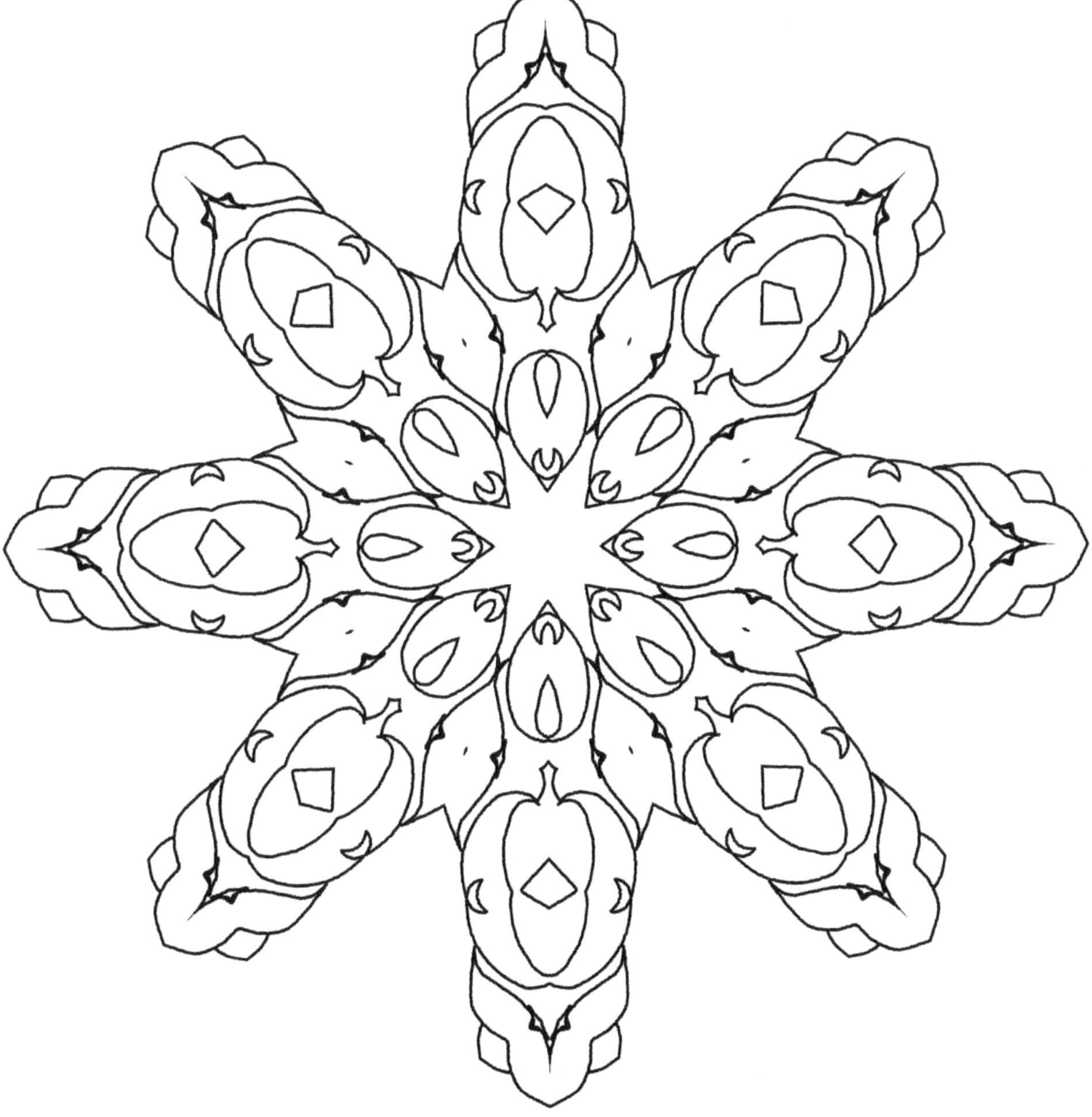

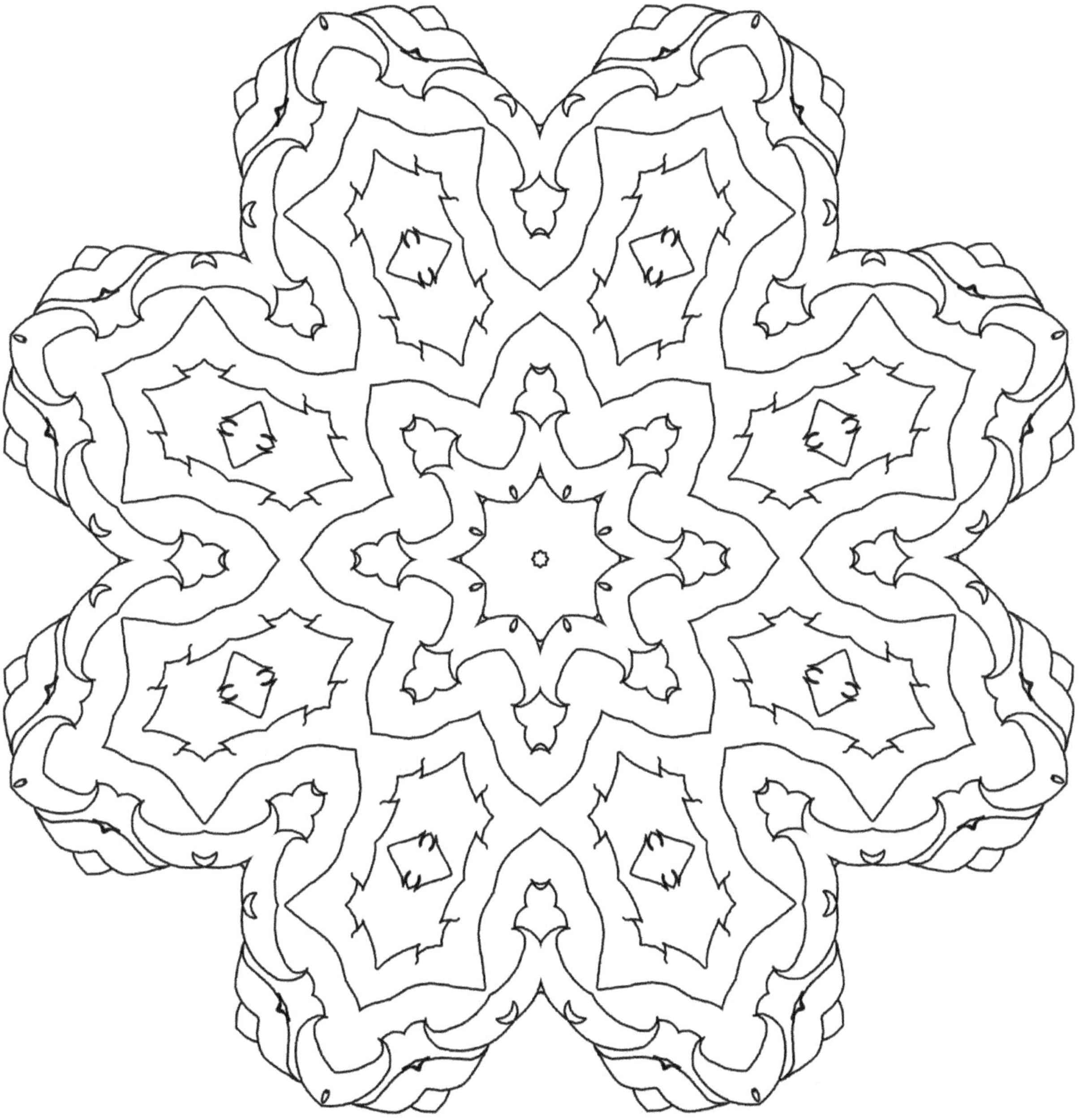

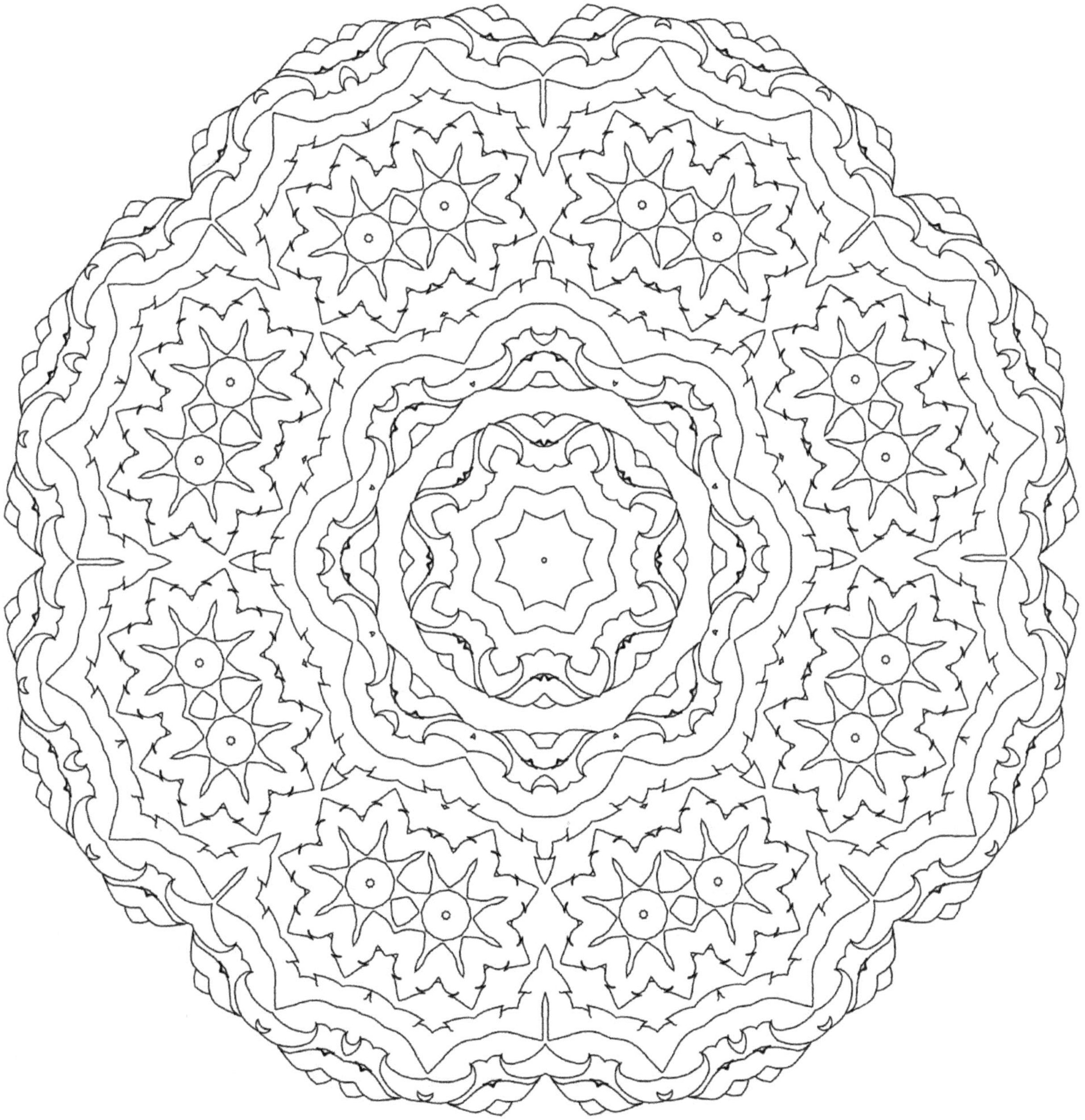

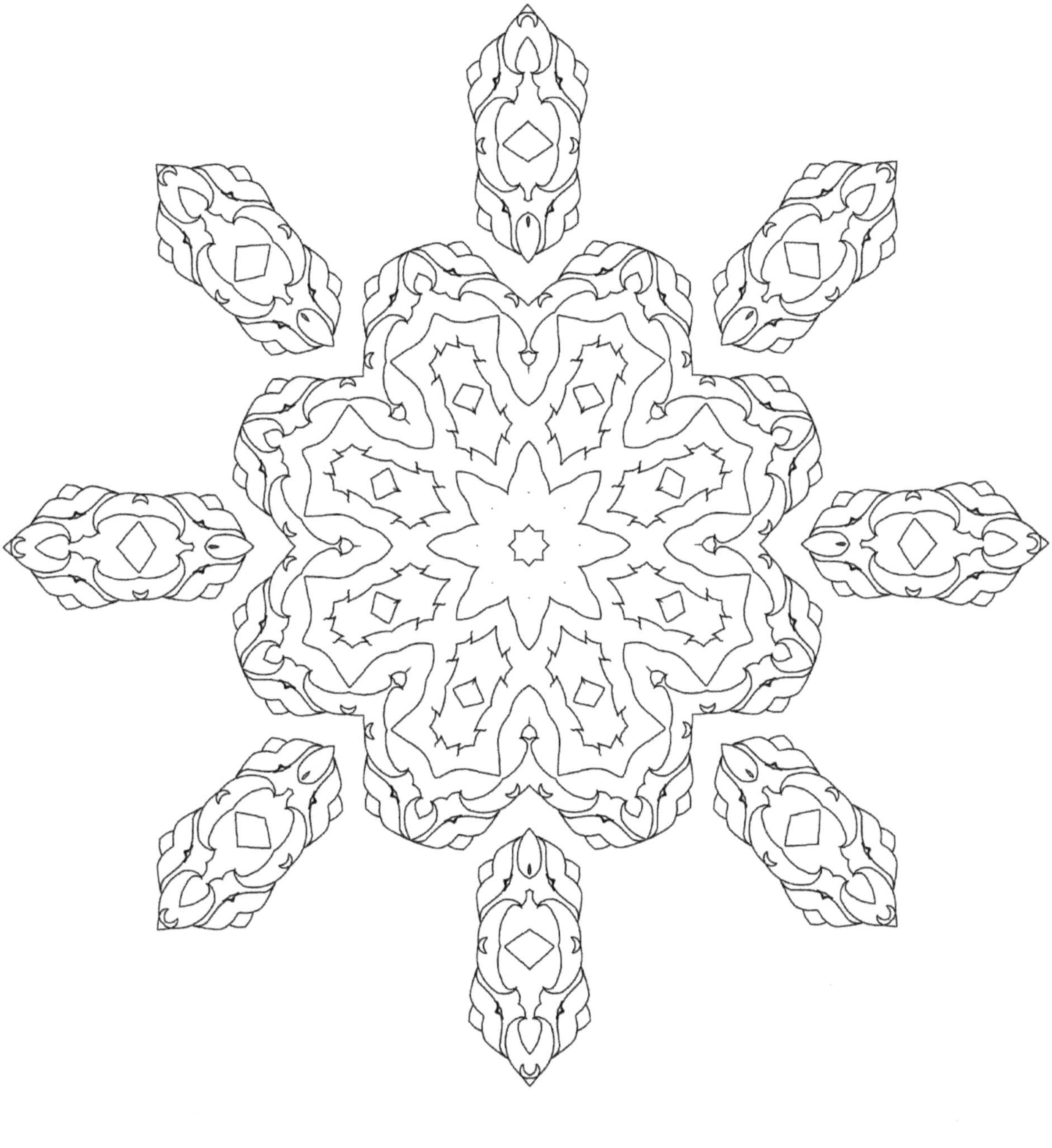

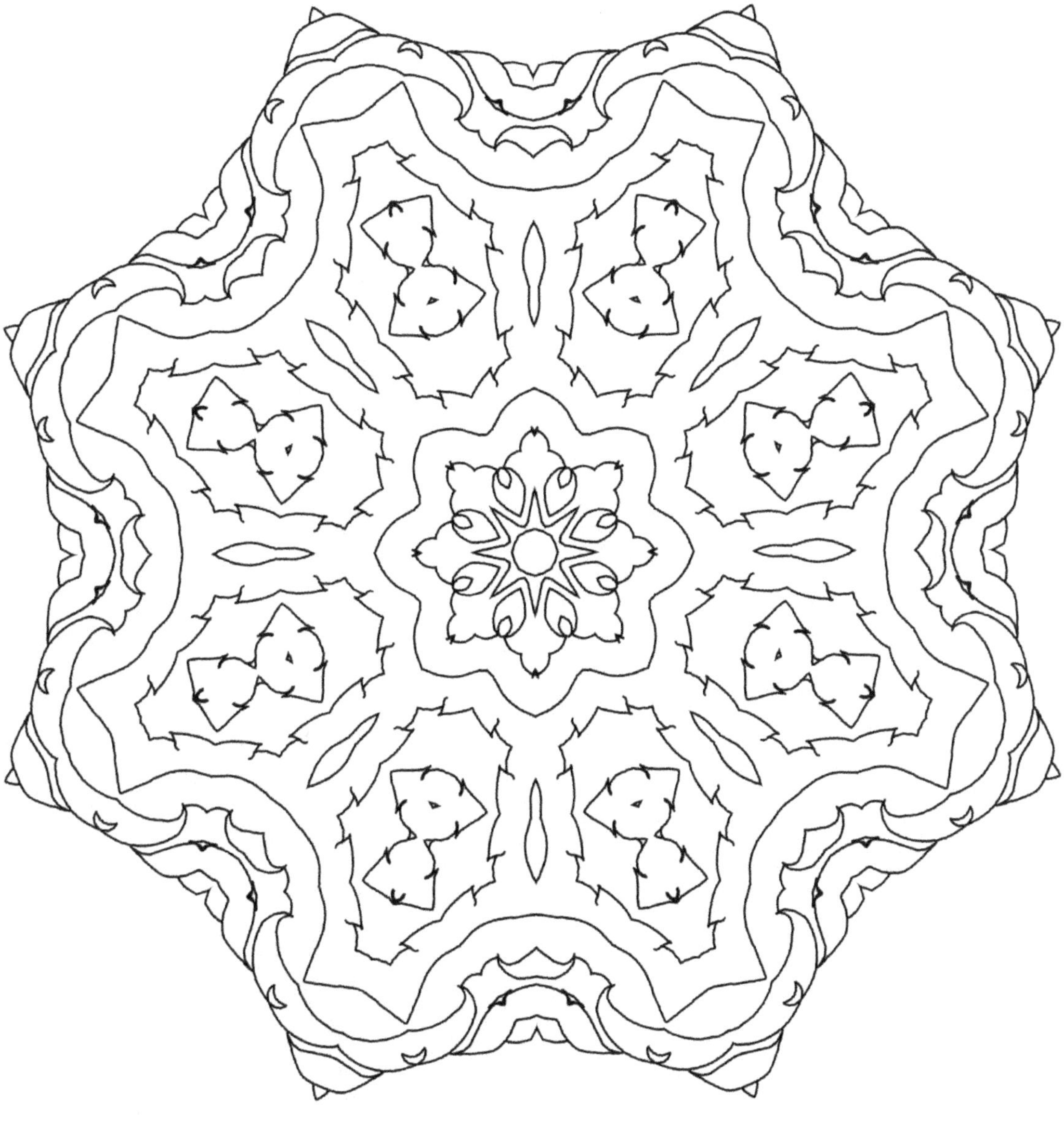

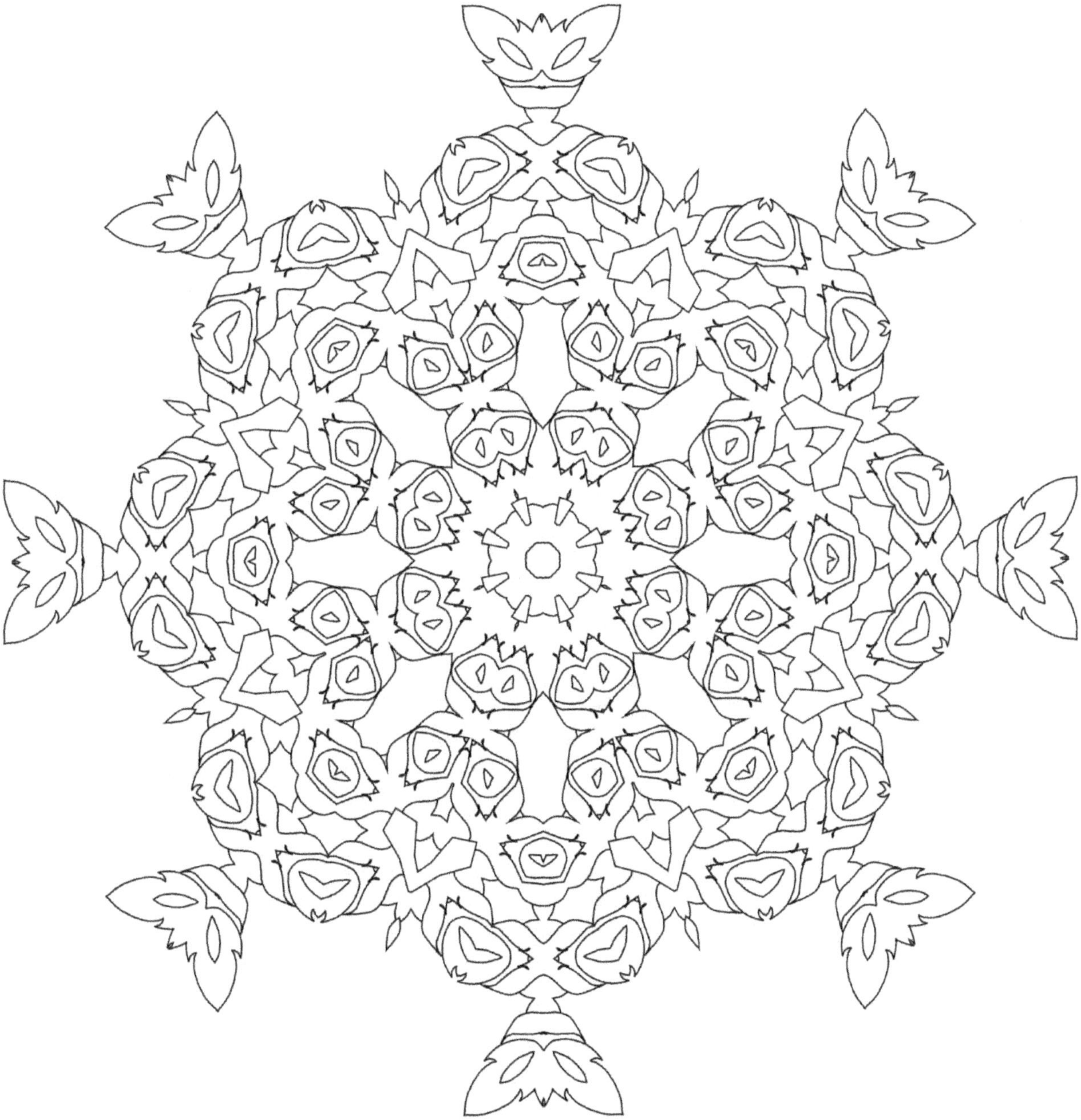

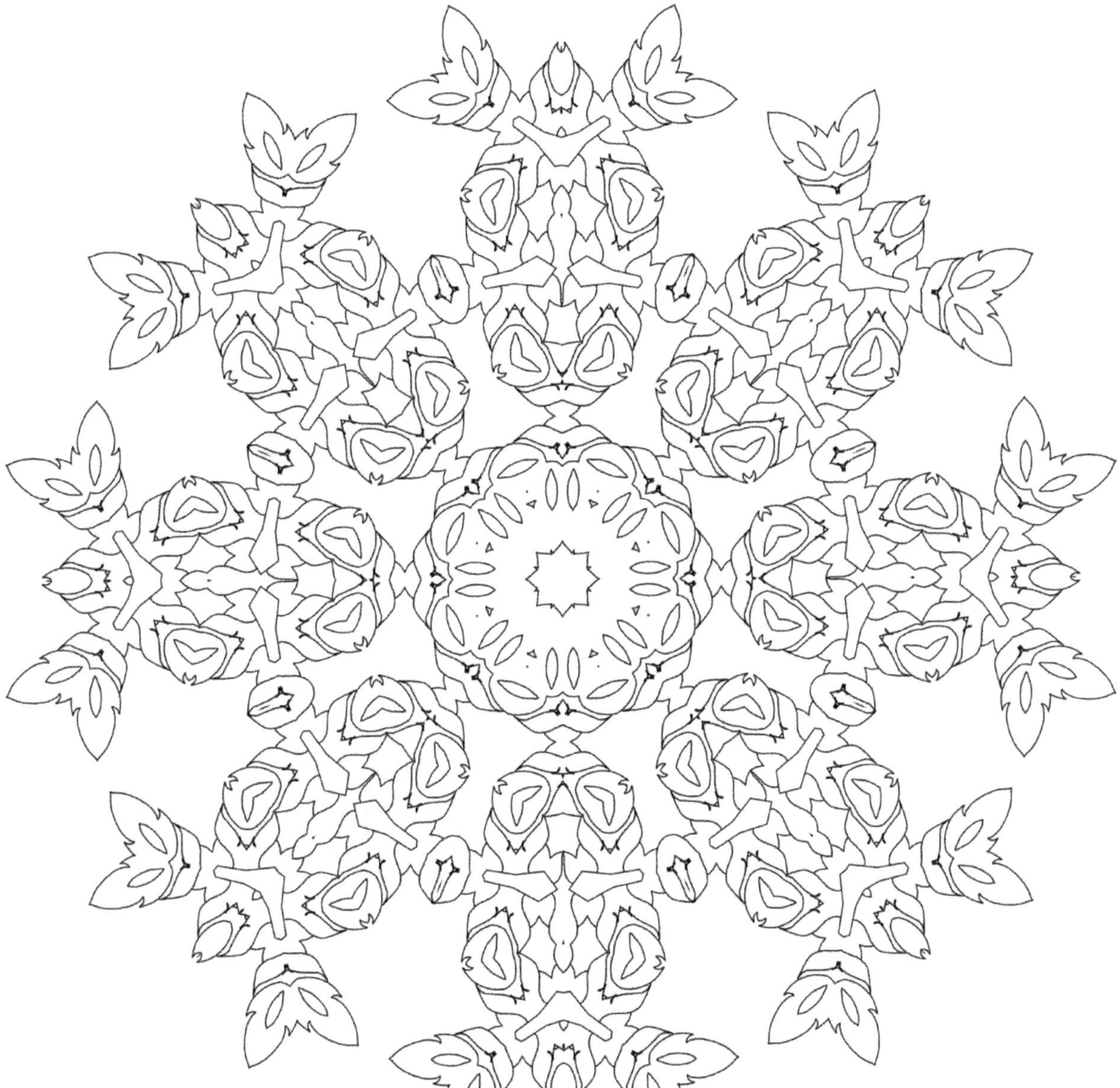

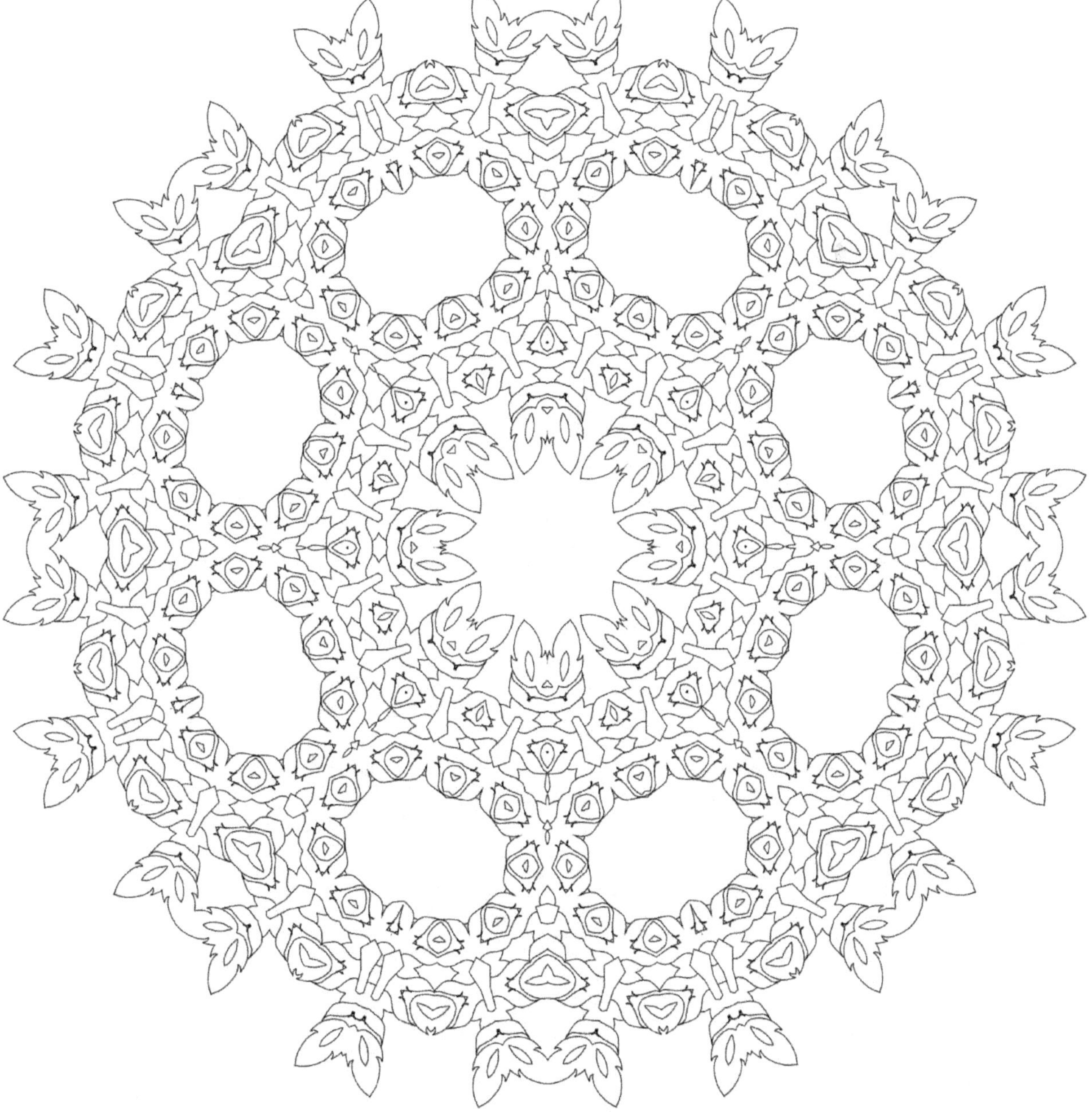

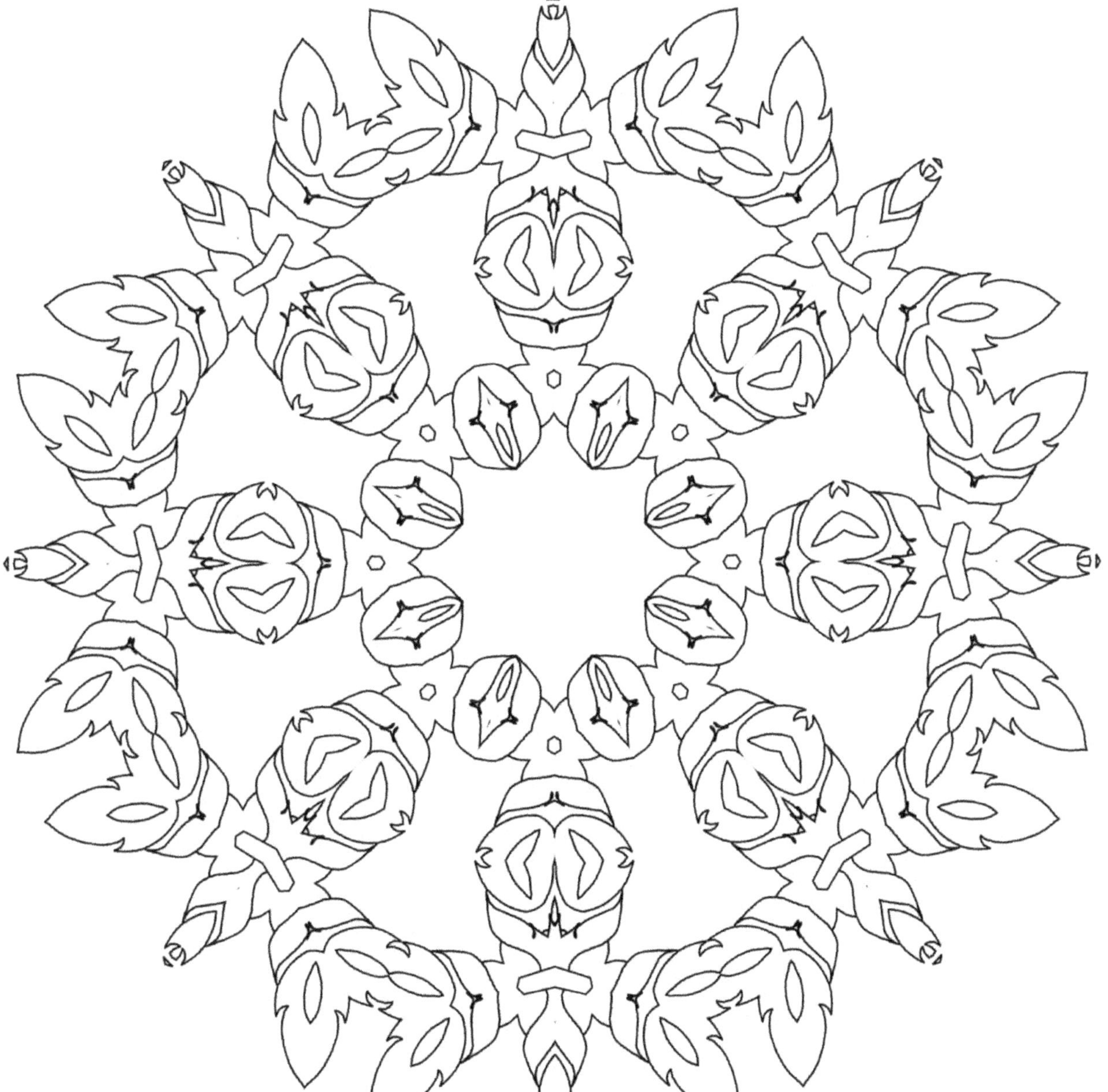

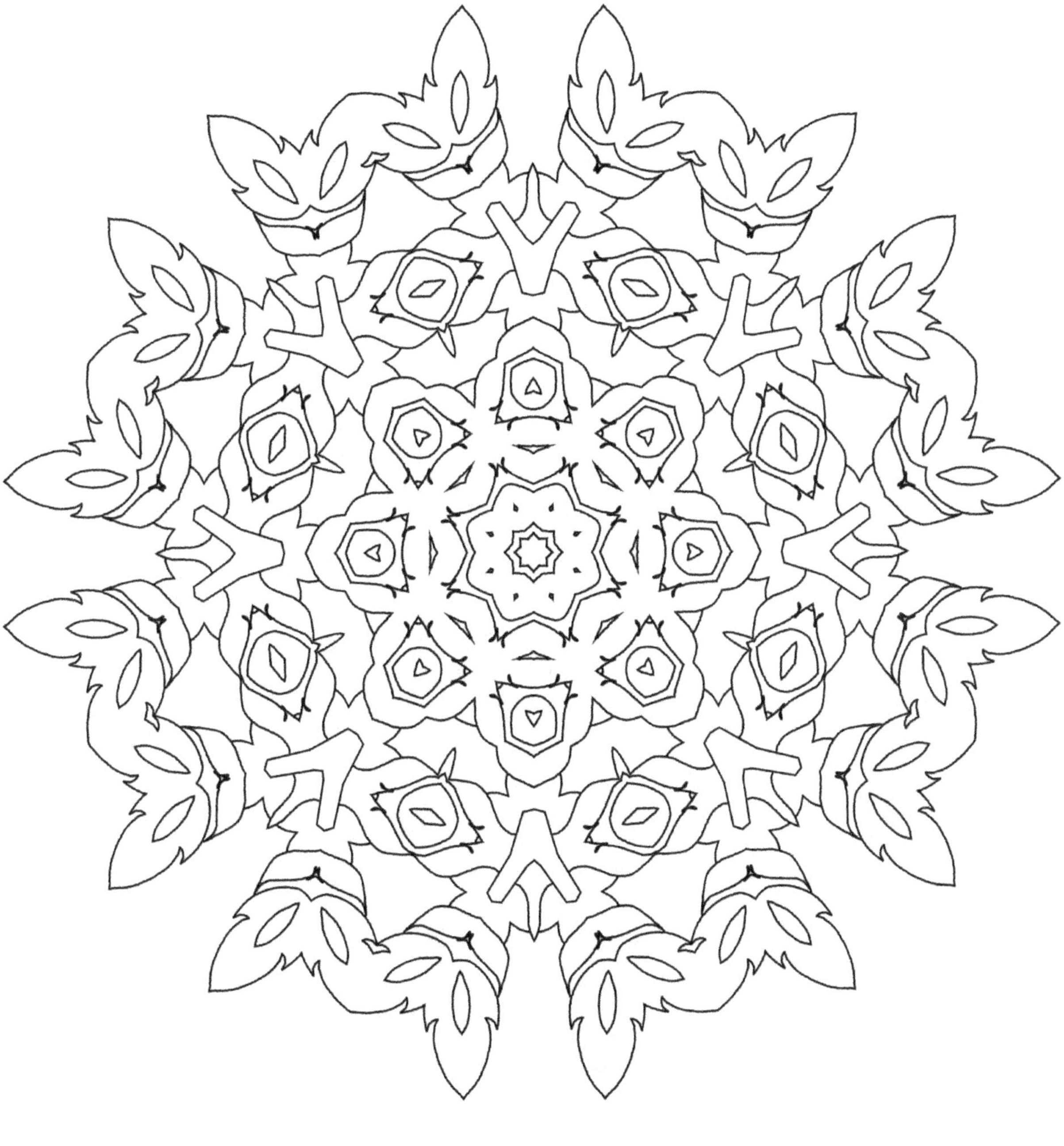

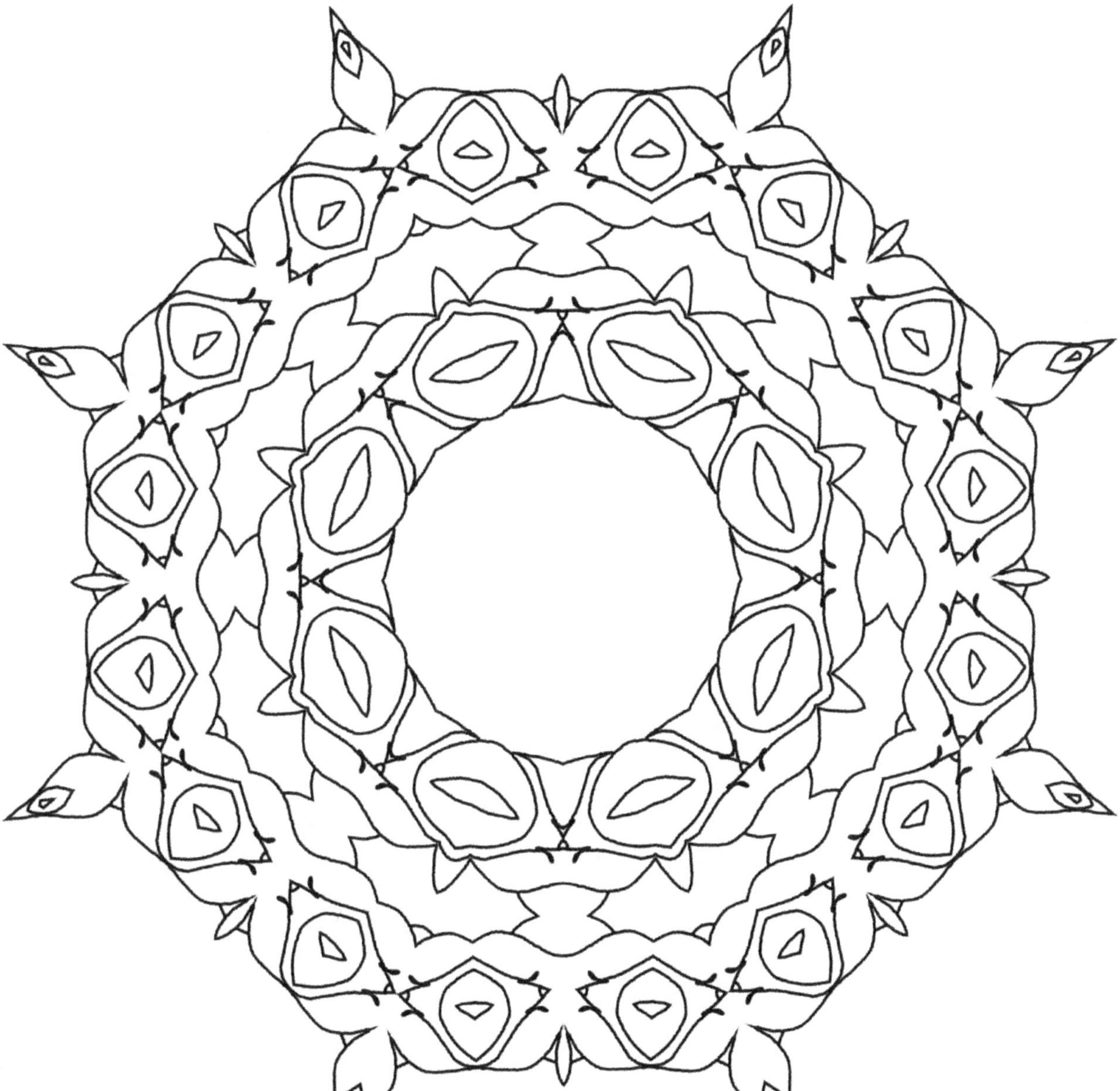

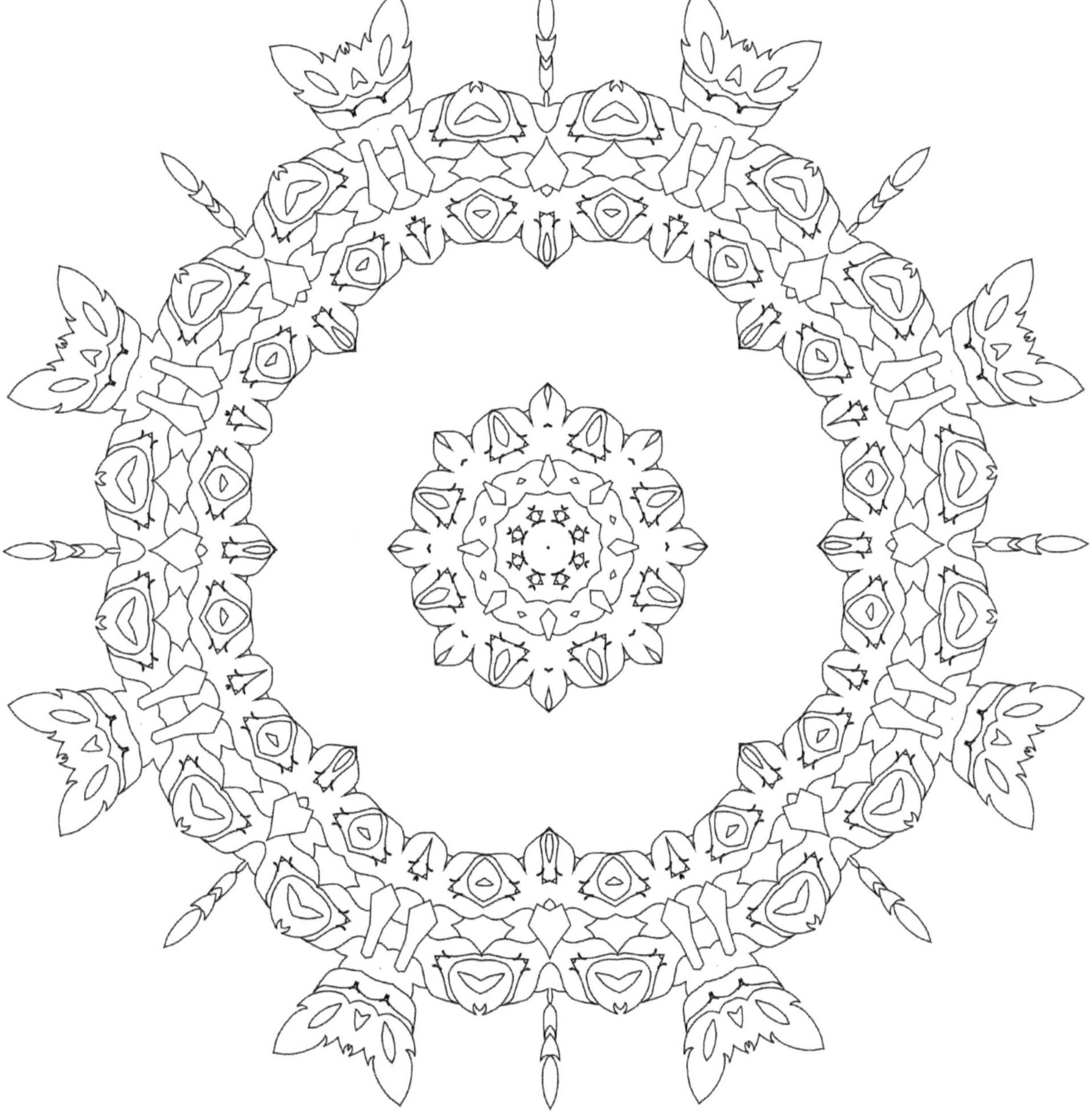

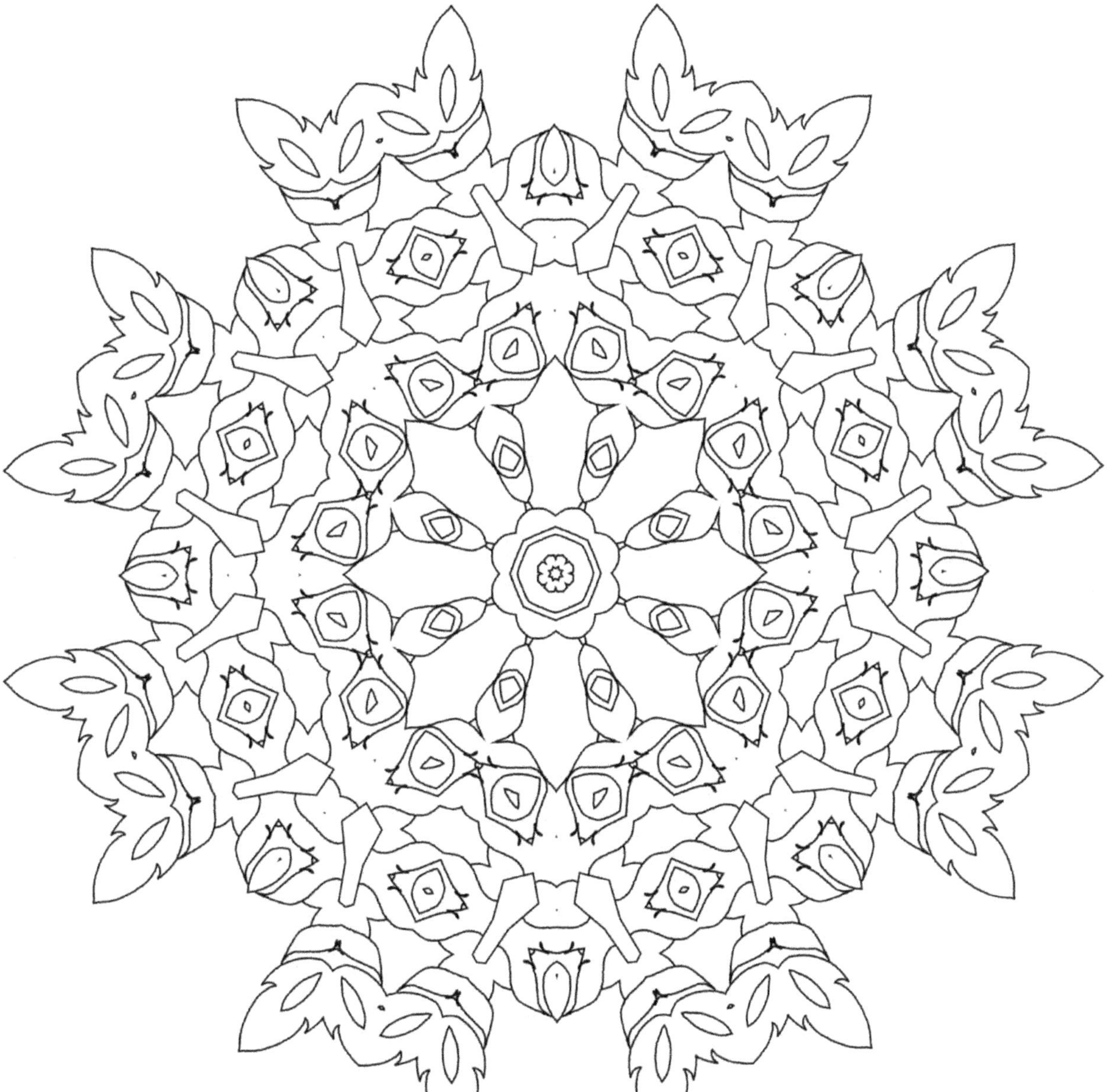

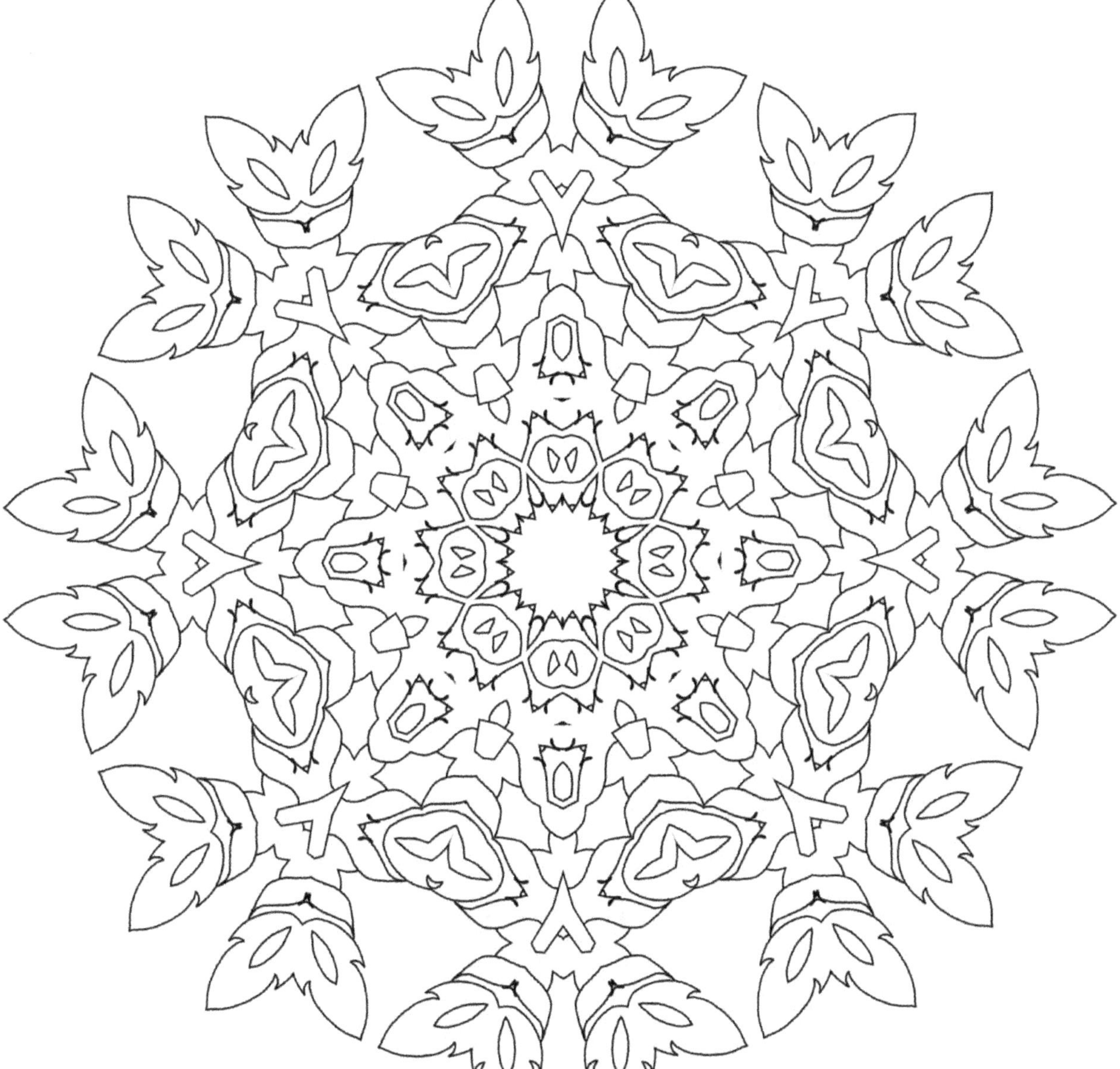

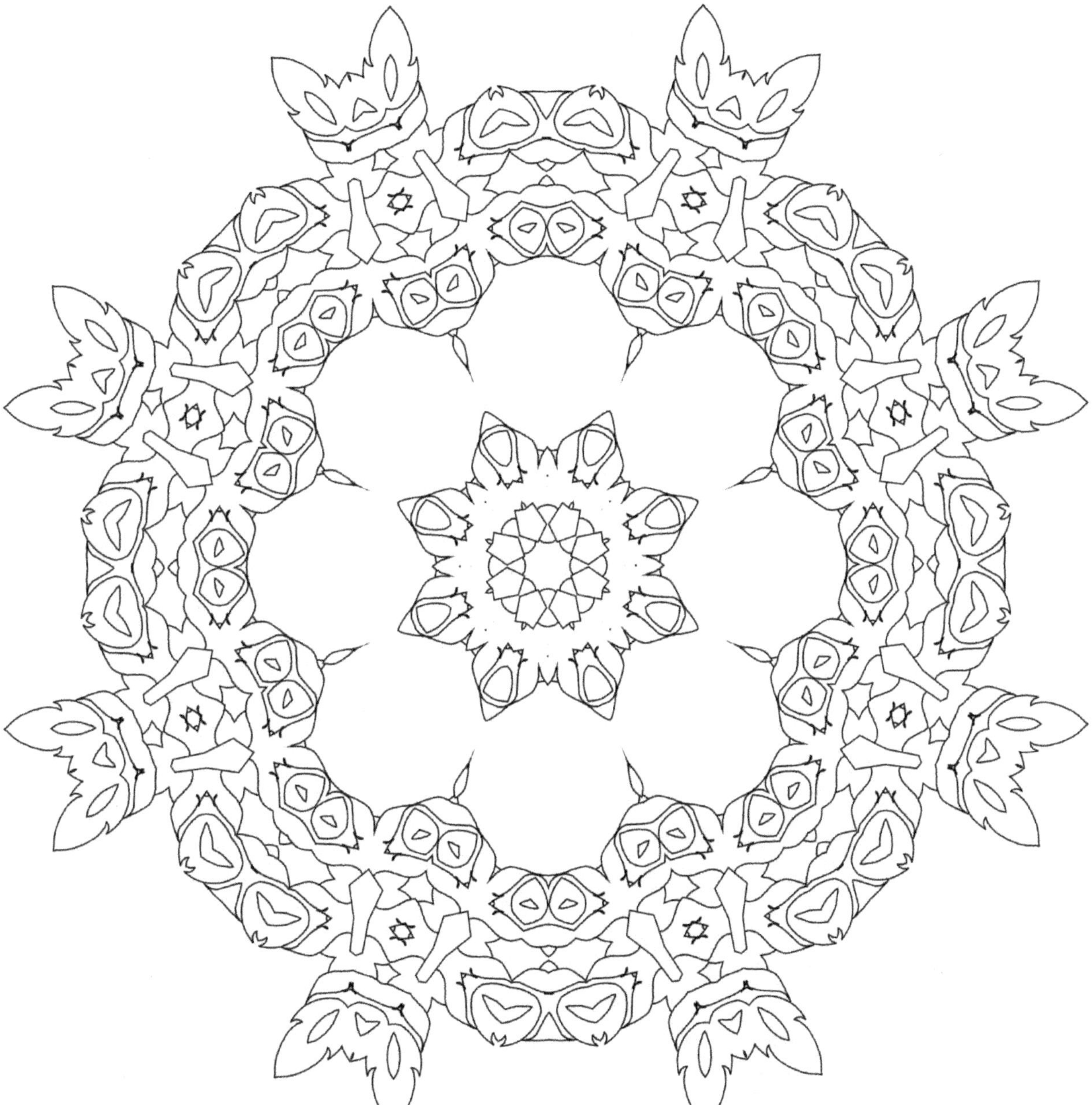

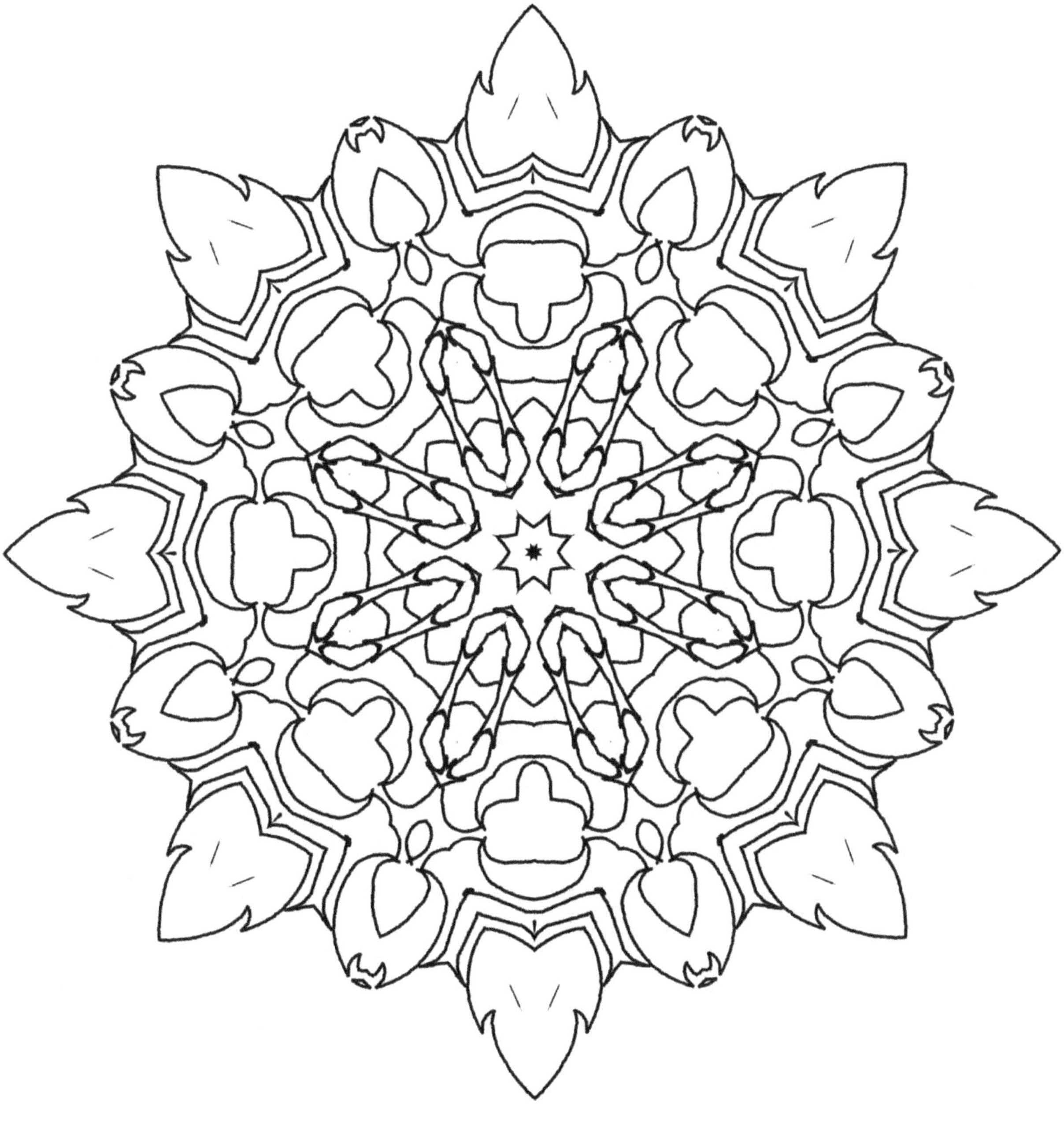

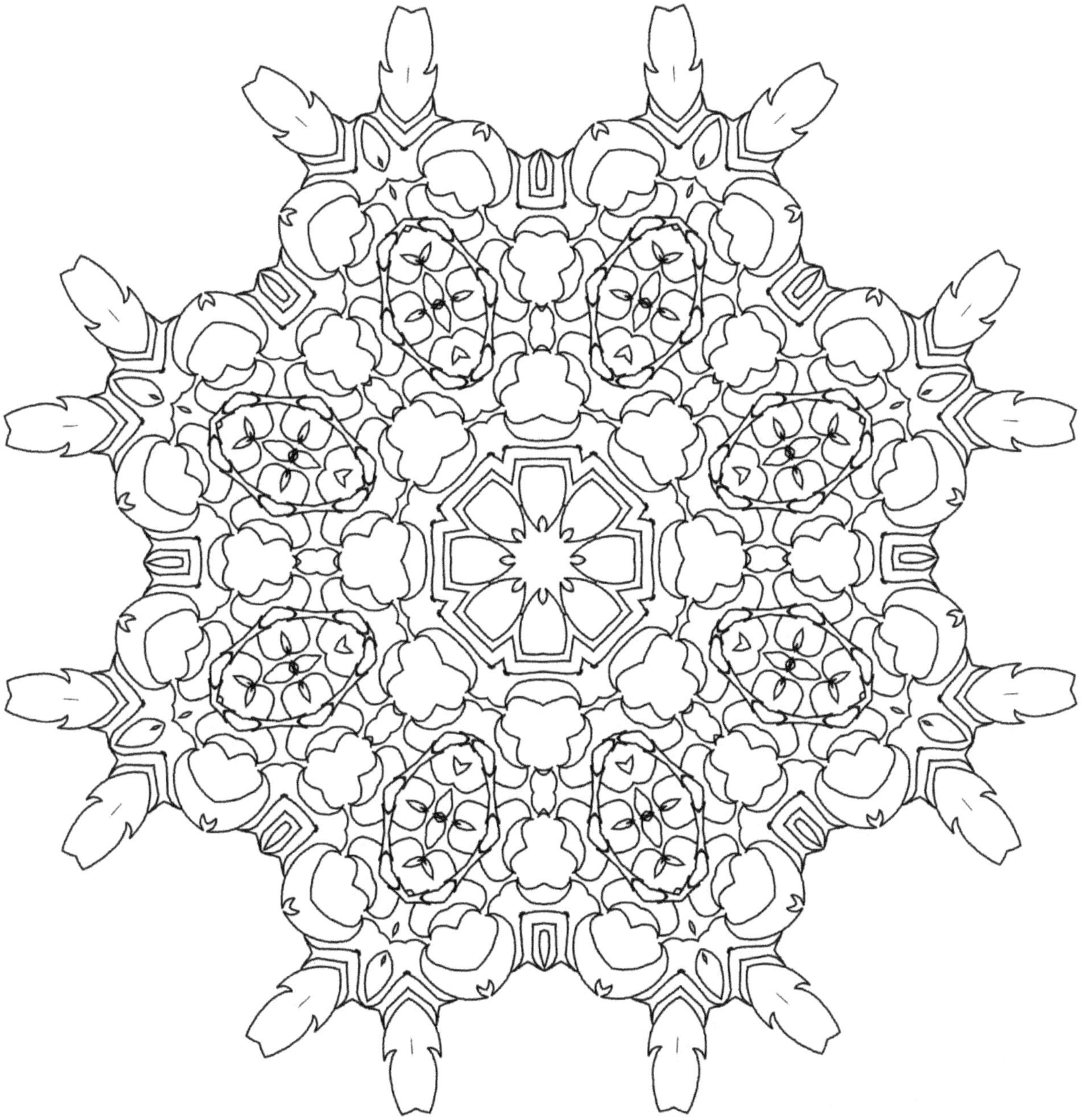

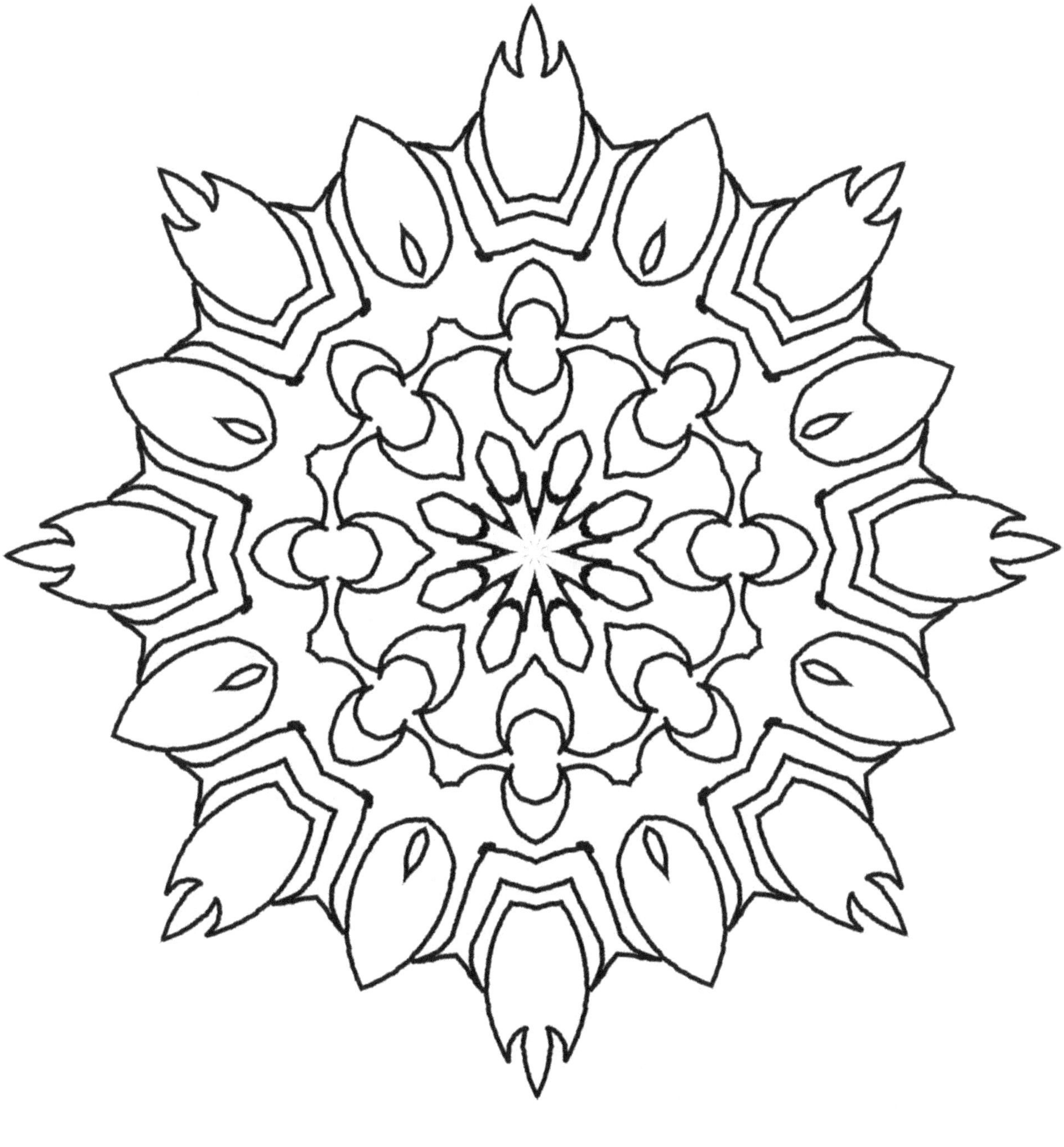

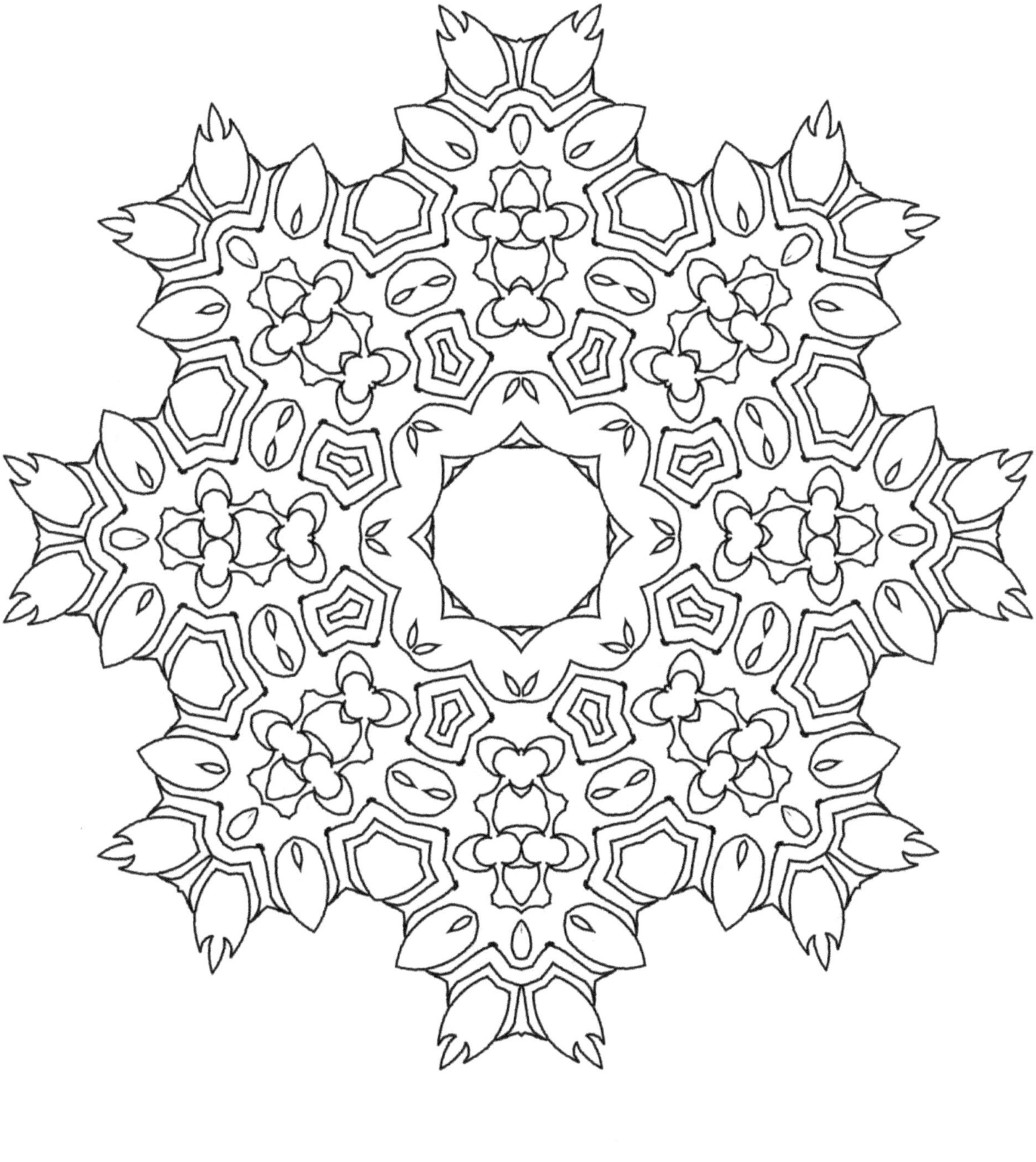

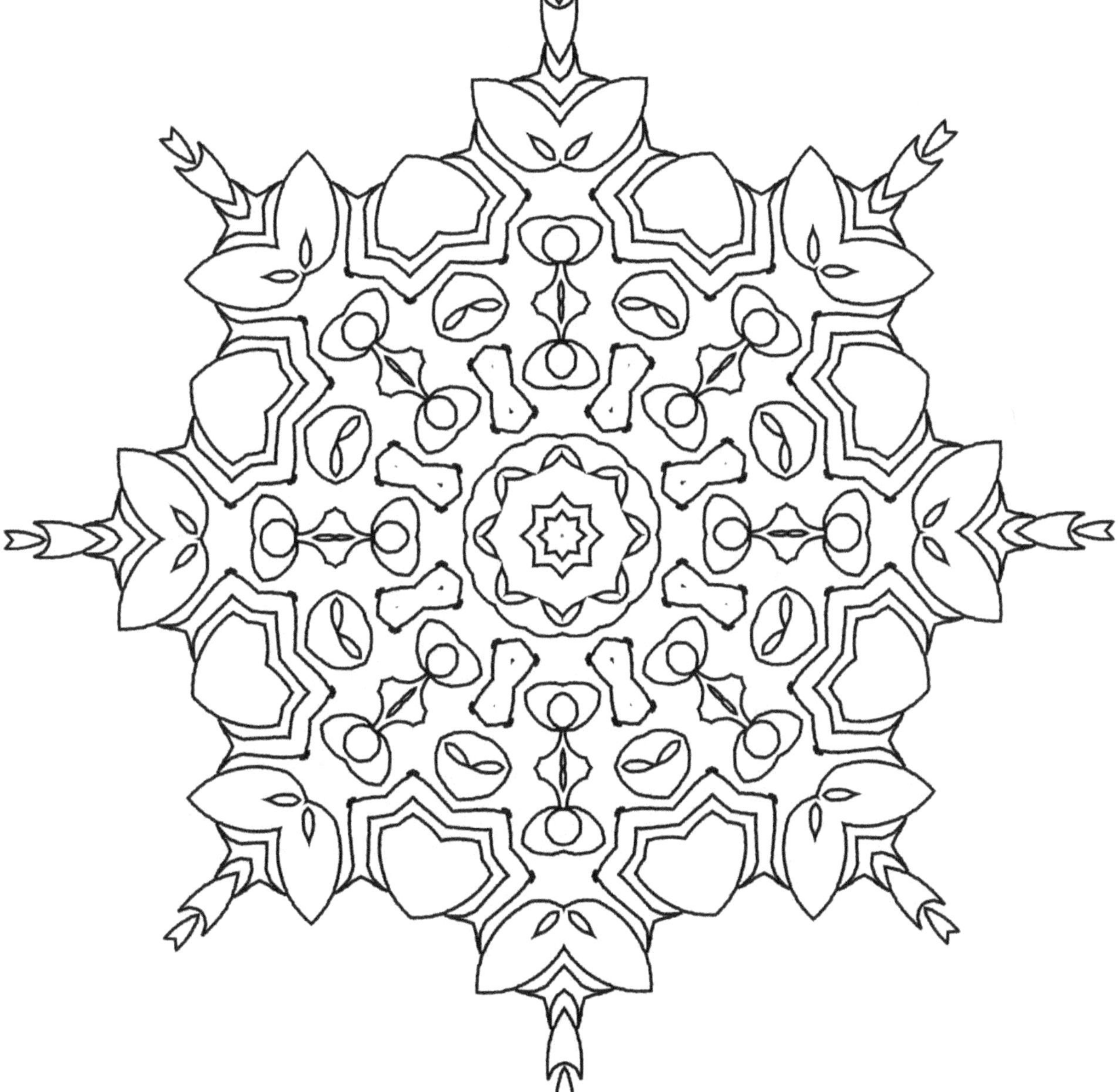

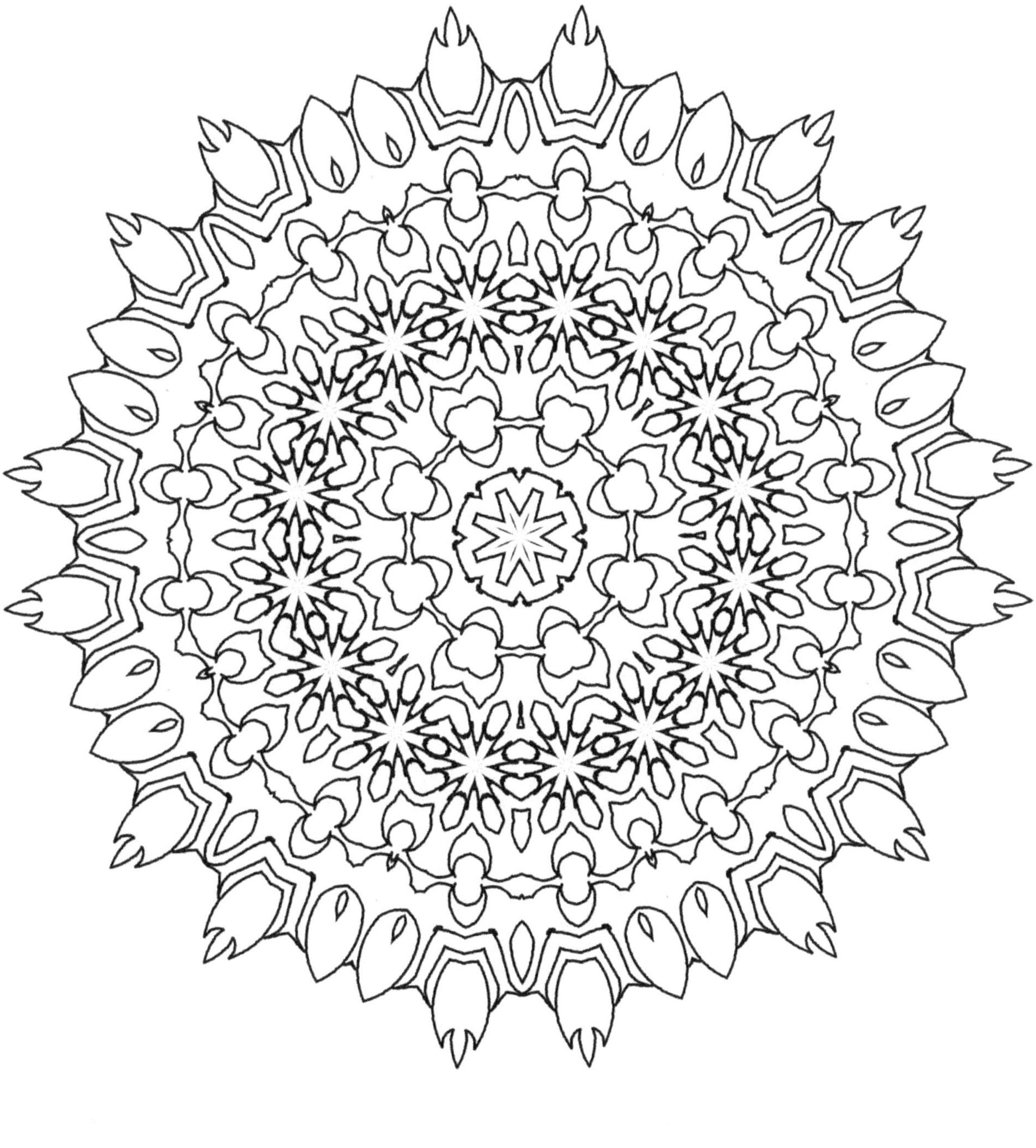

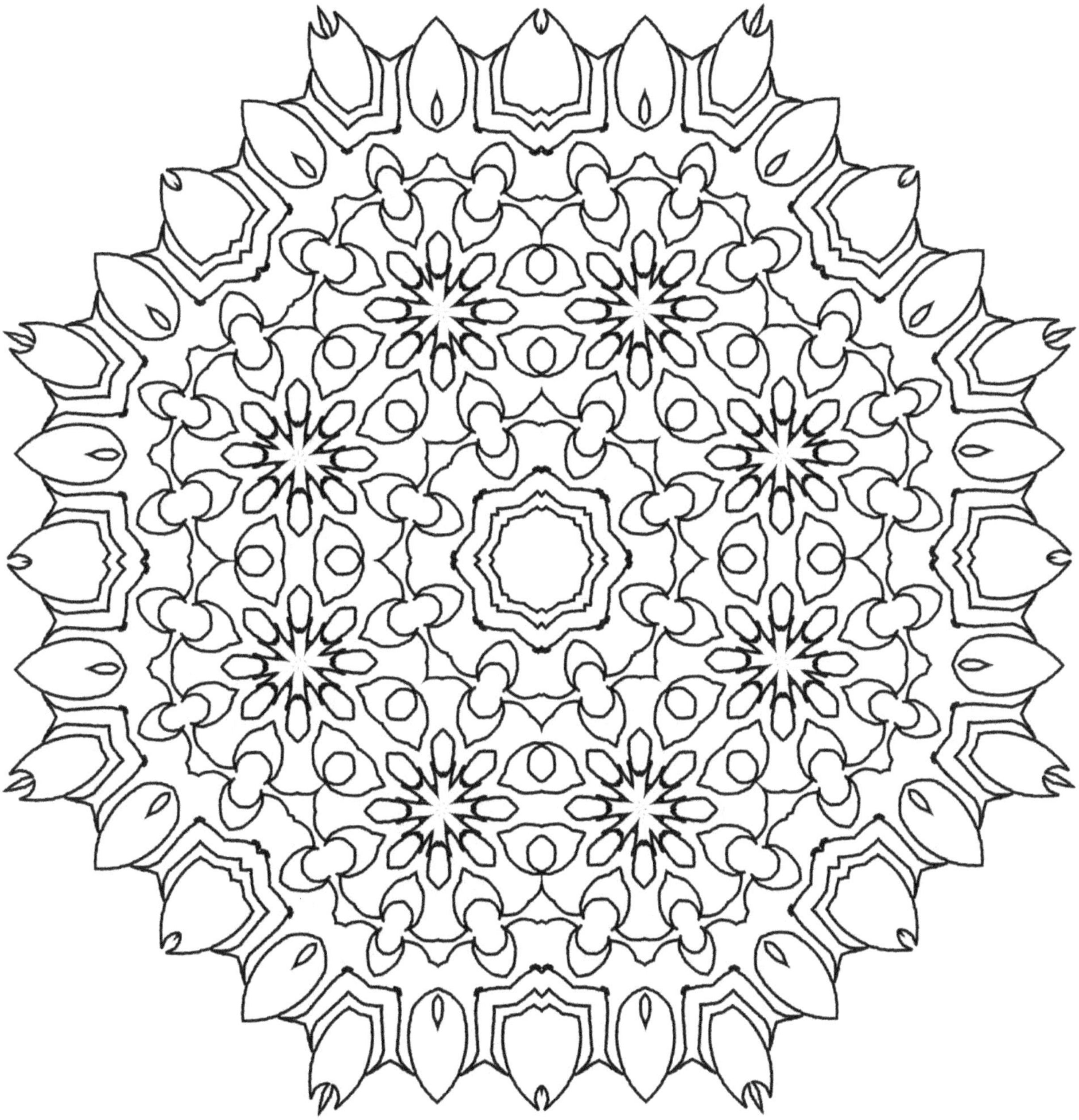

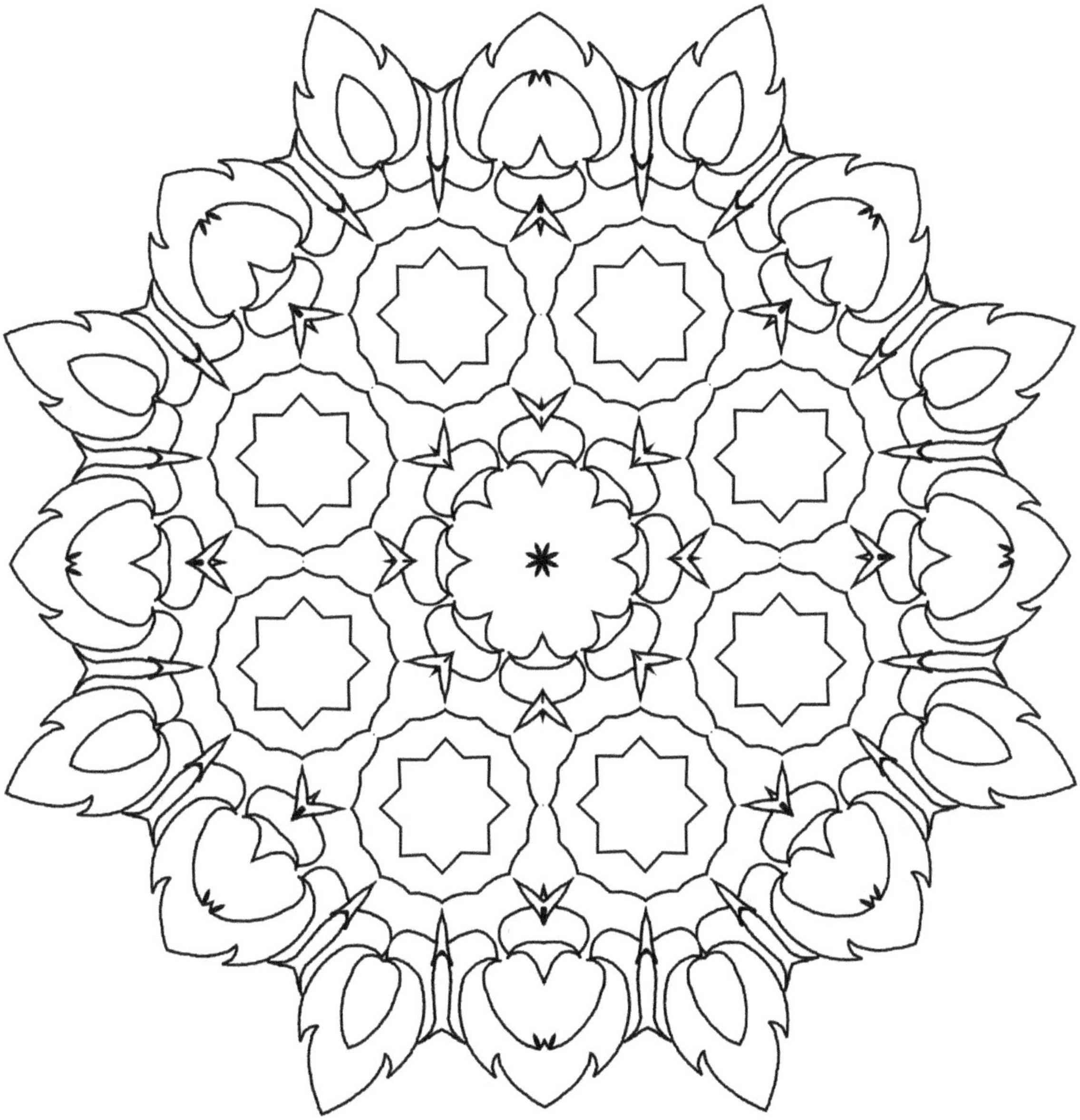

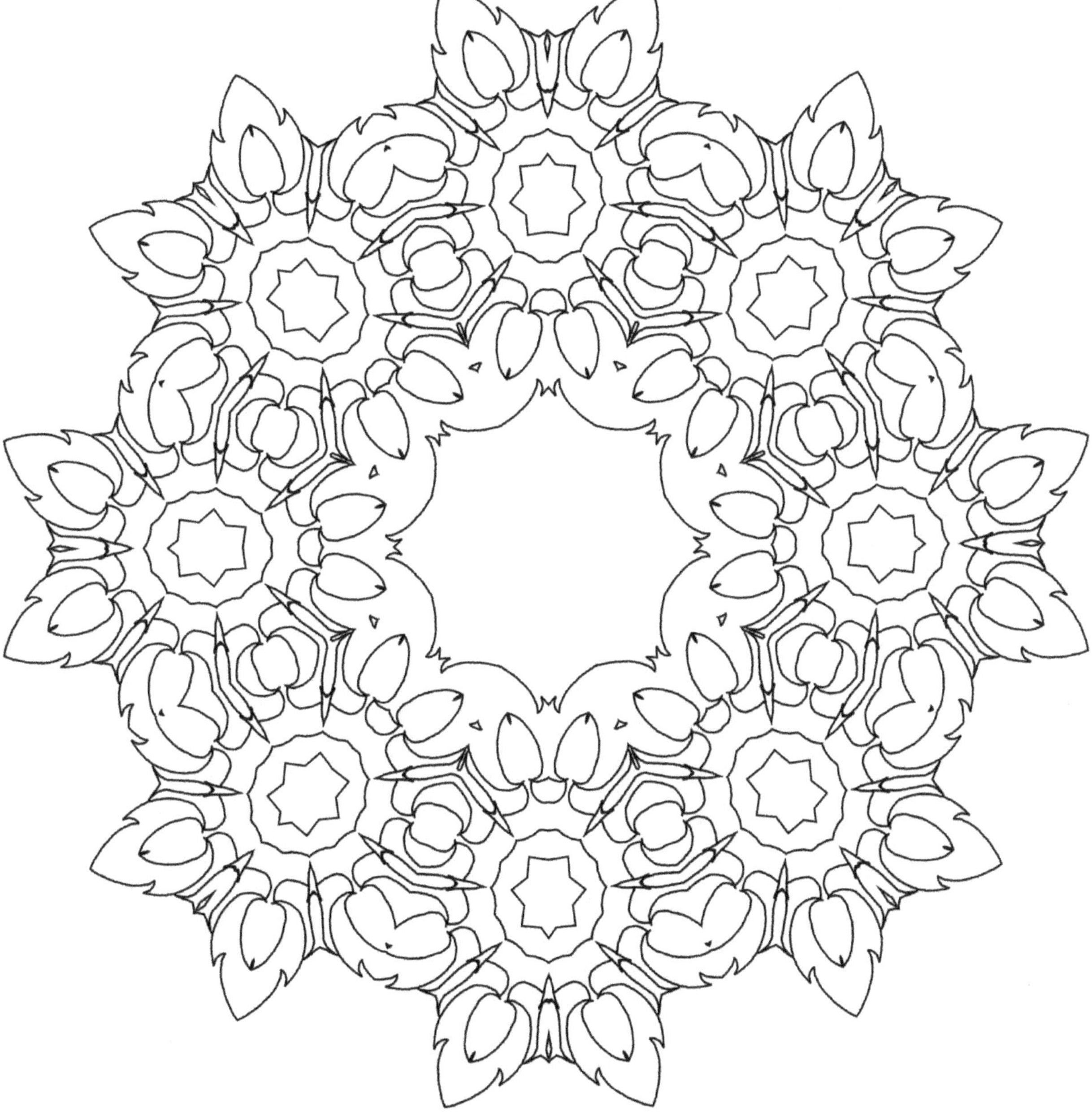

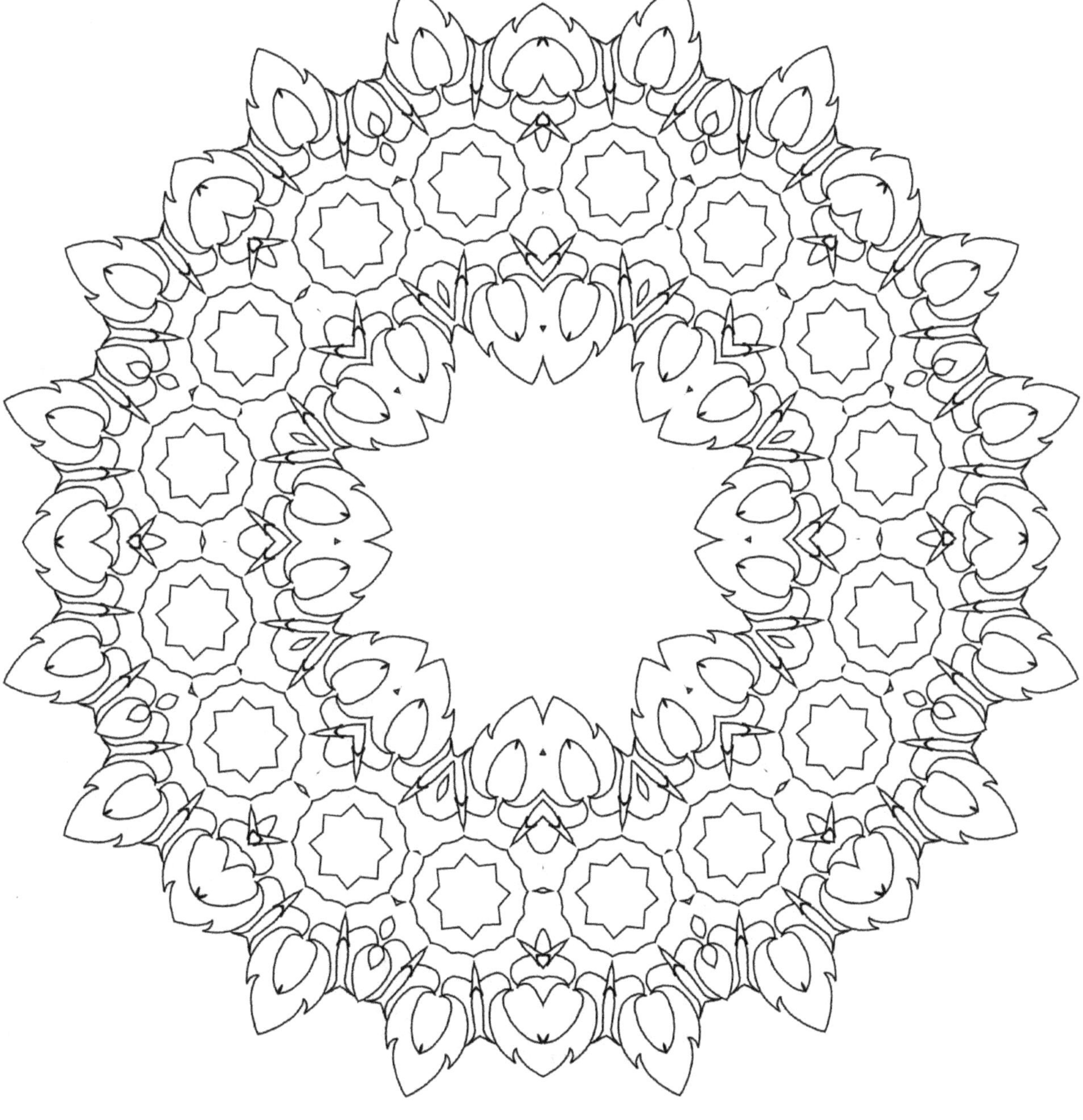

Thank you

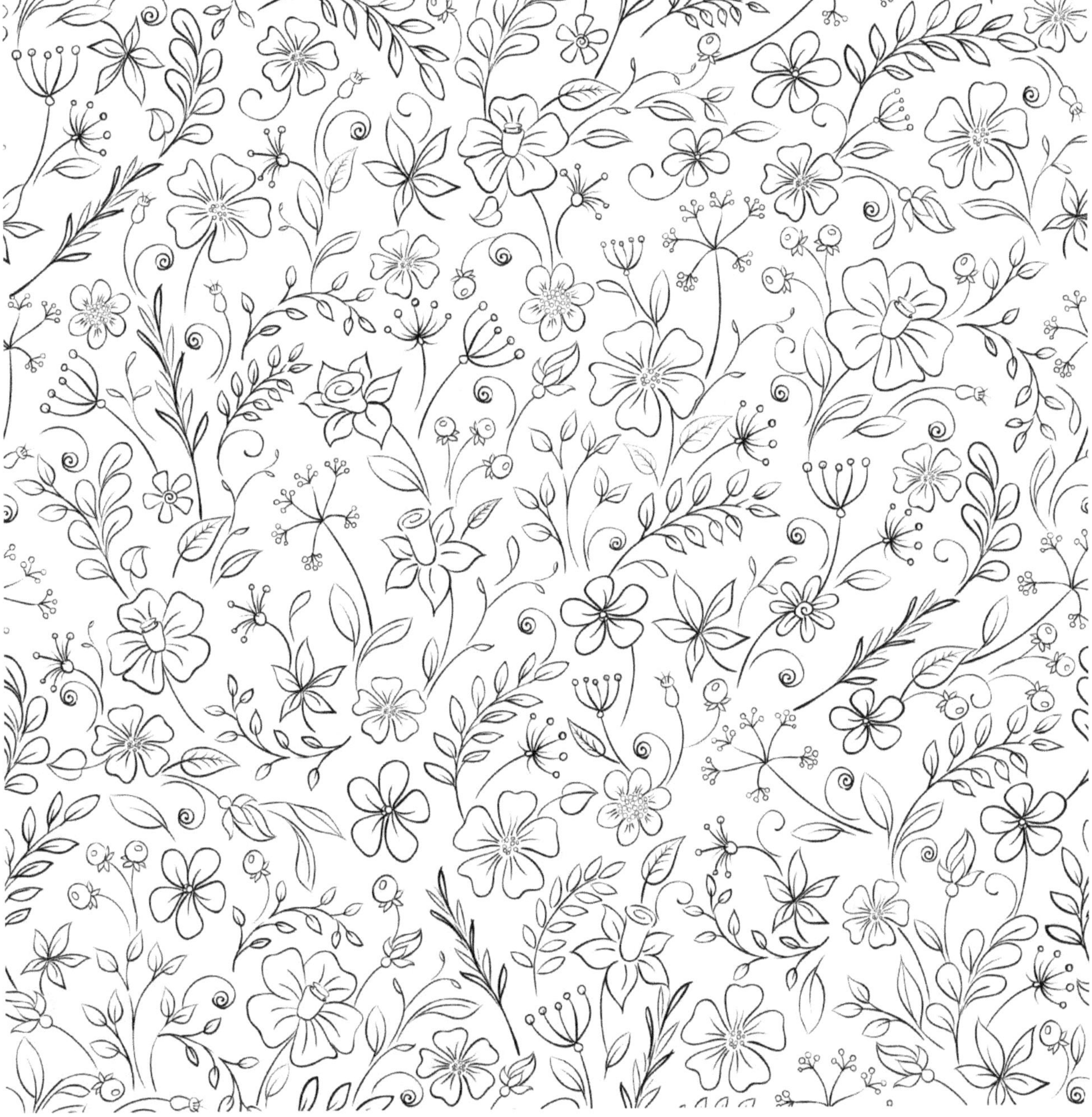

www.ingramcontent.com/pod-product-compliance
Lightning Source LLC
Chambersburg PA
CBHW081117180526
45170CB00008B/2882